THE SADDAM DUMP

[Saddam Hussein's Trial Blog]

Scott Rubin

and

MoDMaN

[www.saddamdump.com]

Published by National Lampoon Press

National Lampoon, Inc. • 10850 Wilshire Blvd., Suite 1000 • Los Angeles • CA 90024 • USA • AMEX:NLN

NATIONAL LAMPOON, NATIONAL LAMPOON PRESS and colophon are trademarks of National Lampoon

The Saddam dump: Saddam Hussein's trial blog / by Scott Rubin and MoDMaN. --1st ed.

p. cm.

ISBN 0-9778718-5-1 - $14.95

Book Design and Production by
JK NAUGHTON

Illustration and art direction by
MoDMaN

CONTENTS

[I Am A Good Character] 3

[Why I Didn't Do It] 19

[Why I Did It] 39

[I Bomb Your Freedom] 65

[Don't Believe The Hype] 87

[Here Comes The Rain] 105

[Brass Tacks And Bare Knuckles In Baghdad] 117

[The End Is Near] 135

[The End] 149

THE SADDAM DUMP

[Saddam Hussein's Trial Blog]

THE SADDAM DUMP

[I Am A Good Character]

MORE ABOUT ME

For the first posting I want you to know about me. The "about me" section of my blog does not meet my fulfillment. Therefore it is required to have more, "more about me." – Saddam Hussein

SaddamH
View My Profile

Age: 69
Gender: 100% male
Astrological Sign: Taurus
Zodiac Year: Ox
Industry: Socialist Pan-Arab Tyranny
Occupation: President of Iraq
(*That's right! The president of Iraq–FU! MFer!*)
Location: Undisclosed, Iraq
(*C'mon, who are we kidding? I'm in the Green Zone*)

Saddam is like God. Saddam is the reincarnation of Nebuchadnezzar, ruler and rightful king of Babylonian empire, defender of Palestine and conqueror of Mesopotamia. Saddam is disco.
– *And now she's in me, always with me, tiny dancer in my hand*

Likes: Cleanliness, nice suits, limb piles, paintings on velvet, grandchildren, walks on the Euphrates, biological weaponry, afternoon prayers to Allah, dissenters with blood gushing from their lying treasonous throats, SUVs, Palestinians

Dislikes: Slovenliness, beggars, painted whores, Paris Hilton, parking tickets, counterfeit antiquities on eBay, Jews

Interests include:
- Provoking the greedy, empirical, halfwit president of America (I cannot even write his name because I am shaking with anger. I wish he would call. I could make it better)
- Manipulating international economy
- Fucking with the French
- Drinking with Putin

Saddam is Disco

- Taking bribes
- Giving bribes
- Blogging
- Polishing scud missile
- Disputing territorial boundaries
- Pumping oil
- Facial hair

Favorite Movies: *Dirty Harry* ("What's it going to be, punk? Go ahead make my day." LOL, the best comedy ever!!)

Favorite Music: Albums: Saturday Night Fever Soundtrack, The Best of Gloria Gainer. Other songs I like: Psycho Killer–*Talking Heads*, Kiddie Grinder–*Marilyn Manson*, Prison Song–System Of A Down, O Sole Mio–*Placido Domingo*

STRENGTH IS POWER

POSTED BY: SADDAM H.   AT 4:12 AM   (852) COMMENTS   PERMALINK ✉

Comments:

Hey Pinhead, you know what? You are a joke! That's what you are – a joke. And you're a criminal for committing crimes against humanity. And you hate freedom and justice. After 35 years of running a country with no judiciary, save for trials that were prejudged by you, Iraq is totally unprepared to conduct this trial. So I tell you what, why don't you just do the same thing you did to those thousands of innocent people you slaughtered and sentence yourself to death right now, and save us all the trouble. That would be a funny punch line... you joke!

Listen, when this thing blows over, love to have you on *The Factor*. The ratings will be huge! Call me.

Posted by: NoSpin_Bill

Please remove my site from your Friend's Links:
http://www.JacquesChirac.com

This is embarrassing.

Posted by: ChiracDaddy

---

view more comments

An Abomination To Islam

Daily Trial Entry:

I am forced day after day to take part in this American puppet court of justice while they have me sitting in a pigpen.

A PIGPEN! The American Crusaders know that Muslims are revolted by pigs… it is the ultimate insult. As a Muslim man, to sit in a pigpen is a disgrace!

In other Crimes Against Humanity trials, defendants were treated with much more respect. Adolph Eichmann, the Nazi Death Camp Doctor, was given a glass booth. He looked like a dignified banker taking a deposit, or that illusionist David Blaine about to transform himself into a mighty tiger. I, on the other hand, am made to look like a pig!

I will not show up unless my surroundings are made stately. I would prefer a small stage with a curtain… Here I may sit in pensiveness on a fine velvet-covered throne, as I consider the trial like your King Lear. And, if they are scared that I will launch into a contemptuous pronouncement of my innocence, they can close the curtain – Bah! I am Saddam Hussein! My people love and respect me!

STRENGTH IS POWER

POSTED BY: SADDAM H.   AT 5:31 PM   (0) COMMENTS   PERMALINK ✉

comments

The Great Armies Of Satan Speak

Note To Self:

How the great armies of Satan are asking for my advice. Take this recent email:

> I'm Corporal Brent Hollister with the US Army 5th Regiment stationed in Ramala. The other soldiers and I have been monitoring your blog with great curiosity. As a platoon commander, I've found it extremely harrowing trying to maintain order in your country. It appears that no matter what we do, the Iraqi people are intent on killing us.
>
> We've given them free elections, empowered their women, built schools and Kaboom! Limb Chowder! I don't remember roadside bombings when you ran things.
>
> I know some experts say it's because we don't know the Iraqi customs, or don't speak the language. Okay, so what is my translator supposed to say: "Hey, excuse me, can you extinguish that lit fuse? You know, the one that's sticking out of your butt, before my balls become part of your brain pan." For God's sakes I'm on my 8th tour of duty. I signed up to the Ohio National Guard. I thought at worst I'd be plowing snow or helping out during a hailstorm. It was supposed to be just weekends for Christ's sake!. I've been here like 3 God damn years and there's no end in sight. My wife is fucking my best friend's neighbor, I'm missing my big toe and left kneecap, and I'm one of the lucky ones. This thing is never going to end!
>
> For the love of God, you are the only one who can control these people!
>
> – help

Yeah, that was pretty funny.

STRENGTH IS POWER

POSTED BY: SADDAM H.   **AT 6:14 PM**   (0) COMMENTS   PERMALINK ✉

comments

Where The WMD At?

Musings:

I am getting tired of being asked, "Hey, Saddam where are the WMDs?" What did Bush think he would find: a giant steaming vat of glowing green ooze waiting for him in a warehouse in Falluja?

No, it doesn't work that way. You spread it around. A small vial of anthrax strong enough to take out a city... you put it everywhere. It's in Ahmad's house, and Fareed's house, it's in spray canisters and bike tires. I sent a batch FedEx to Cleveland. It's like hiding the contents of a couple of pixie sticks from your little brother. Biological is so easy. I could never believe Bush actually thought he would find these.

The missiles? Right in front of your nose: they hold up bridges, they are the large flagpoles, pillars in my palaces, and the minarets in our mosques.

The chemical weapons are in Thermoses at our 99-cent stores, in urns of our dead soldiers, and in all Walmart vases. It's really that easy.

STRENGTH IS POWER

POSTED BY: SADDAM H.   AT 8:04 AM   (3) COMMENTS   PERMALINK ✉

Comments:

Hey, where's my $20,000?! I blew myself up, and my family is still waiting to collect.

Achmed Pala, Palestinian Suicide Bomber, 7th Level of Hell

Posted by: Notta_limb_onme77

view more comments

Slept In ... Blamed Lawyers

Daily Trial Entry:

First, here's one of today's headlines:

. . . .

Saddam Stays Away As Trial Resumes, Misses Graphic Testimony
A woman described being stripped naked and hung by her feet while Saddam
Hussein's half brother kicked her in the chest until her ribs cracked. A former Baath
Party guard said...
—Washington Post

. . . .

I know what you're thinking, and I can explain.

My alarm didn't go off, and by the time I got myself composed and ready for
the day, it just seemed such a waste. I phoned the courthouse and said that I
wasn't feeling well. But the judge gave me a very hard time, so I told him the
whole thing was a farce (again) and blamed the lawyers for being
incompetent and unprepared. Blaming the lawyers seems to have worked
pretty well

— I ought to write that down. It might be useful.

STRENGTH IS POWER

POSTED BY: SADDAM H.   AT 9:21 AM   (0) COMMENTS   PERMALINK ✉

comments

Lunacy Requires An Iron Will

Note To Self:

I've decided that a solid trial strategy should include evidence of my good character. I get such a bad rap from the Western press, WMD this, and tyrannical dictator that. Of course I had to put up a "gruff" exterior. How else could I maintain control with all the lunatics who live in my country? I mean, have you seen that self-flagellation thing they used to do down in Umm Qasr every year? Holy shit! That's one thing I put a stop to a long time ago.

A parade that features hitting yourself on the head with a sharpened piece of sheetmetal can only lead to trouble.

But I digress. If only the court and the international press could see my true nature, they would see that I am a peaceful and benevolent leader who loves to shower his people with kindness. If they could see Saddam's inner, more gentle, self, they would know that I should still be the rightful ruler of Iraq. For example, did you know that I write poetry? Well I do, and here is one that I composed just this morning.

A Bug in my Cell
By Saddam Hussein

Warmth of sunlight streaming
Through the window of my cell
Morning with no reason

A bug appears
Finding comfort in my forearm hairs black and gray
How much we share in common this bug and me

I too am in the wrong place
Oh bug. Please bug, be my friend
Oh bug you want to fly, such disappointment

Ahh, it stays!
Stay with me my little friend and I will provide for you

Oh bug you have left me!
In flight now – to the bars, to the air
I reach for you, such yearning

Oh bug you are taunting me!
Deviant bug, come here this instant or you shall pay!

I have you now, firmly in my grasp, ha, ha
I have tweezers, now your head is gone
I pluck a dingle berry from my arse
Now it is down the bloody stump that was your throat

You son of a Kurdish whore!
No more will the bug disobey me
Meaning and hope have been restored

STRENGTH IS POWER

How Much Is Too Much Stuff?

Musings:

I can't help but wonder – have I put too much emphasis on my personal belongings? I mean, can a man have too much stuff? You don't need clutter in your life... Be picky.... Did I really need to hold onto my first bicycle, clay busts of myself without my moustache, and a large box of tongues? Some of this can surely be thrown away or donated to a silent auction for charity. Too much shit is too much shit. All of your most valued possessions can be easily stored in two or three medium-sized palaces.

Nobody really cares about your stuff when they enter your house anyway. They are measuring themselves up against you and are too self absorbed to appreciate the wonderful artifacts of your life... most are thinking *"Why don't I have gold plated toilets?"* instead of marveling at the framed sword used in your first beheading. If you must hold onto things, museums are a much better place to display your possessions. Call your local curator and tell him you'll come down with a few items if he would make a special exhibit or two of your life. They usually agree to do this, but you must have the right tone in your voice.

Remember you must *impose*; do not ask.

STRENGTH IS POWER

POSTED BY: SADDAM H.   AT 5:47 PM   (13) COMMENTS   PERMALINK ✉

Comments:

I was on Joe Scarborough's MSNBC show last night, part of a panel discussing whether President Bush should be impeached. You might have caught it ... I don't know what time it comes on over there. Anyway, as I always do in any political debate, I started out the evening arguing about Bush's imperial and illegal adventure in Iraq. This always results in blank stares and heavy sighs, which is my cue to look smug and claim to have won the argument. Works every time.

Speaking of legal, this might be good for your current "situation."

BTW It's great to see you've started a blog – good for you! Maybe you'll consider linking to my blog??
http://www.huffingtonpost.com

Hit me back and let me know.

Posted by: PrincessArianna

Dude@#$%@#!!$# — I thought we had a deal??

– You suck

Posted by: U.N.Koffi

I am the real Saddam Hussein. The person they have in prison and who is writing this Blog is in fact not me. I am writing this from another location. I am free and often play with pigeons. This monkey they have in prison is a stooge, a body double that I used to open Baghdad Shopping Malls in the 80's. He's an idiot. He would constantly show up to the wrong stores at the wrong time. He couldn't even cut a ribbon properly. Once he accidentally cut a testicle off of the manager of a Pearl-in-the-Oyster pagoda. Do you think the elected leader of Iraq would ever stoop to the nonsensical defense strategies that this moron has put forth? I went to college. I ascended to the very top of the Baath Party. Do you have any idea how difficult it is to rise to the top of Iraq when virtually everybody wants to kill you, including members of your immediate family? To do so takes intelligence and a cunning that this babbling idiot could only wish for.

Do you think Saddam Hussein would be caught dead in that $10 suit, or not shave every day? This son of an adulterer should be found guilty and hung at once. He is an embarrassment to me, and the Iraqi people. Like Napoleon, I shall return once the American oppressors learn that I am the only one who can manage the Iraqi people.

Posted by: Saddam0001

---

view more comments

Never

Daily Trial Entry:

I have been assigned a new group of defense attorneys. I am an educated man and respect bright legal minds. But some of these lawyers were assigned to me by the Iraqi puppet court run by the Americans. These are spies at best! I will not work with them, never!

Actually two of them aren't so bad. My defense will be simple. I will yell and scream, then I'll not show up, and when I show up I will continue to yell and scream.

STRENGTH IS POWER

POSTED BY: SADDAM H.   AT 4:28 PM   (0) COMMENTS   PERMALINK ✉

comments

Can't Sleep

Note To Self:

Giant Pig Plushy… I can't stop dreaming this image. Is it the pigpen?
Something is going on with me. I've been visiting furry fetish sites. Is there
anyone out there who can make this happen for me? I went on Ebay today
and they would not allow me to set up an account. My name is blocked.
Please, I must wear the Pig Plushy. I have hidden gold & WMDs. Perhaps I
can make a trade on craigslist.

Oh, God! Will this nightmare never end?

STRENGTH IS POWER

POSTED BY: SADDAM H.   AT 1:41 AM   (0) COMMENTS   PERMALINK ☒

comments

Freedom Awaits

Daily Trial Entry:

Today is a glorious day, my brothers. My trial is getting back on track. They claim that I murdered many Iraqi citizens after a failed assassination attempt on my life. I did not. My lawyers inform me that on that day I was attending a shopping mall opening in Baghdad.

STRENGTH IS POWER

POSTED BY: SADDAM H.   AT 5:59 PM   (0) COMMENTS   PERMALINK ⊠

comments

Soon To Be Free

My attorneys just left and confirmed that I am, in fact, a body double.

STRENGTH IS POWER

POSTED BY: SADDAM H.   AT 12:10 PM   (14) COMMENTS   PERMALINK ✉

Comments:

Praise be to Allah who created the creation for his worship and commanded them to be just, and permitted the wronged one to retaliate against the oppressor in kind. Peace be upon him who asks — Does the crocodile understand a conversation that doesn't include a weapon?

Miss you :(

Posted by: O_SammyB

Hi, I'm from Mark Brunett's office, and he asked that I pass this onto you, so I'm posting it here. Hope you get back to us...

Saddam – Wow, do you have any idea how good you are?! You're amazing: ruthless, but yet surprisingly funny and sensitive. There's definitely a show here. Your eccentric strong-arm methods would make great television. Here are some quick pitches:

Suicide Justice: This one's simple: You're looking for your next defense attorney. Will they quit, be thrown out of court, get kidnapped or have their throats slit? A great weekly strip.

The Butcher: Each week, 12 wannabe tyrannical dictators battle it out to become the next ruthless despot, while you decide who lives and dies. Who will be the next "Butcher"?

The Henchman: How long can an average, executive assistant, survive the whims and fury of a diabolical leader of an oil rich Middle East country?

These are just concepts. I'm extremely open to suggestions. Let's get together and talk... no power lunch, just real casual.

Posted by: BurnettBoy

---

view more comments

THE SADDAM DUMP

[Why I Didn't Do It]

I Have Suffered At The Hands Of The Infidel

Daily Trial Entry:

Another partial truth by the international press:

. . . .

"I have been hit by the Americans and tortured," Saddam told the court. "Yes, I've been beaten on every place of my body and the signs are all over my body."
– Al Jazeera

. . . .

This story fails to tell the unspeakable torturous activities done to me by my American guards. No beatings could ever compare to the American psy-ops torture I had to endure.

It was just another Sunday, when my guards, who I believed were my friends, rolled out a TV in front of my cell. They were laughing, holding beers and eating some sort of chips. I thought we were going to do something new and fun. But they tricked me. I was forced to watch this thing called the Super Bowl. They said it was a great American sporting event.

I have never felt my soul so dampened to the point of extinction. The endless time between plays, relentless instant replays from every angle, no one moving the ball, constant penalties with a video review that questioned the rule of law on the field – never have I seen such insolence in a sporting event. One team, named the Seahawks, had uniforms that were the same color as the field, which put me into some hypnotic, hallucinatory trance. Only the sight of Jessica Simpson throwing Pizza Balls, and the Nacho Cheese Doritos that my guards occasionally allowed me to snack on were enough to resurrect my soul for a brief moment.

My American guards demanded that I stay conscious just long enough to witness the halftime show. They said it was my last chance to see Mick Jagger. I saw a man about my age run around a stage half naked to some primitive rhythm. I was revolted. What Iraqi secrets must I have revealed by this 2-minute warning? Only Allah knows. It was four and a half hours of endless monotony. I would rather be bound and have my testicles wired to a Hummer battery.

By the beginning of the fourth quarter, I began to black out. They told me to snap out of it and finish the game. They said the fourth quarter is always the best part, and that all the action was in the fourth quarter. They shook my chair, as I screamed in agony – *No more! Please no more!* And then, like a miracle, some Pittsburgh player pitched to another Pittsburgh player who threw the ball for a touchdown, and for a second I was revived. But then it happened, I think it was during the twelfth or quite possibly the fifty-sixth consecutive replay of this touchdown, that I began to violently shake. I fell on the floor screaming and shaking as orange foam with shards of Doritos started coming out of my mouth. I had no control of my body. I screamed, "I'll tell you anything! You want nukes, I'll give you nukes! Just make it stop!" But the guards ignored my screams, continuing to pretend to watch this *SUPER BOWL*.

One of them shouted at me, "You gotta wait! They're about to kick the extra point!" The extra point!? By this time all my clothes had been torn off of me from the shaking. Finally, I grabbed hold of the bars of my cell with my mouth. Holding my vibrating, naked body with my teeth, I tried to reach for my Koran for a final prayer, but thankfully Allah had mercy and allowed me to black out again. When I came to, I was propped-up in a chair with my American guards watching something called the *Post Game Show* — the account of which can not be conveyed on this blog for fear that anybody reading it could be needlessly tortured by reading the description of this unimaginable horror. I blacked out again.

The last thing I remember is my guards trying to revive me by threatening that if I didn't wake up I would have to watch the Pro Bowl. Apparently a torture so evil the guards could not stomach it, as we did not watch the Pro Bowl.

STRENGTH IS POWER

POSTED BY: SADDAM H.   AT 10:22 AM   (151) COMMENTS   PERMALINK ✉

This is absurd. Real thugs love to watch football. It's what we do.

Posted by: RaiderNationFan

This is just another example of your human rights being violated! The imperialist Bu$hCo administration and their Halliburton cronies need to be shown what it means to be a caring member of the hu-man or hu-woman, or hu-transgender race (not that race has anything to do with this).

Posted by: TheMightyPen

I was in charge of the torture unit in your Republican Guard. It is ironic that I am now held in Abu Ghraib prison where the Americans torture me also. I have been forced to watch an entire season of "Joey." – Excruciating.

Posted by: Captain_Hurt

Saddam, I feel your pain. After watching the Seahawks performance I too experienced bouts of projectile vomiting.

Posted by: M_Hollgren

This is Sergeant Sean Fardon of the US Army 5th Regiment, I believe my Corporal Hollister sent you an email about formulating an escape plan, but you did not respond. We are serious. You are the only one on Earth that can keep these people in line. Your methods, although deplorable, work.

Somehow, you can gas, torture and rape your people on a regular basis and it is tolerated by the world. We can't even form a naked pyramid of Iraqi prisoners, put a dog collar on a terrorist, or accidentally drop a Koran without having the wrath of the international community come down on us. Please take our offer. We have next week wide open. Just give us the word.

Posted by: SgtFardon

If y'all can't even watch a football game, then I guess we'll have to add "Being a Big Sissy-Queer" to your list of crimes against humanity.

Posted by: RangerRed

---

view more comments

Crimes And Misdemeanors

Daily Trial Entry:

Today I am accused. It is a minor offense. I shall prevail. I am the innocent man. Here is an article with details...

. . . .

Iraqi Panel Files Case Against Hussein
Deposed Leader Accused In 1982 Shiite Massacre
BAGHDAD — The first criminal case has been filed against former president Saddam Hussein for his alleged role in a 1982 massacre of more than 150 people... Hussein is alleged to have ordered the killings in Dujail, about 50 miles north of Baghdad, in retaliation for an attempt on his life there on July 8, 1982.
– Washington Post

. . . .

This is nothing! You'd think I'd slept with the adopted daughter of my mistress and mother of my children, and then married the child. Now that would be worth getting upset about.

I ask you... Could you get away with murder? Not just logistically but privately, in your own conscience? If you do commit murder and then prosper, where is God?

– In my case: yes, yes, and out of sight out of mind.

STRENGTH IS POWER

POSTED BY: SADDAM H.   AT 6:44 PM   (61) COMMENTS   PERMALINK ✉

comments

I see what you're insinuating, very funny. Nice that you can find humor in the way people choose to live their lives. Are you going to post entries titled Match Point, Hollywood Ending, or Sleeper? Actually, that is pretty funny in a very ironic sort of way.

Posted by: W_Allen

---

view more comments

The Koran — Good

Note To Self:

I shall instruct my council to introduce in my defense as proof of my good character the teachings of the Koran and how they have affected my life and guided my actions. How can a good and learned man of Scripture commit acts that are criminal?

In my early years, I was a secularist–this is true, but I came to know the beauty and power of the teachings of the prophet Muhammad.
– Not the crazy strict Muhammad but a more liberal one; you know the one that allows martinis and 3:00 a.m. booty calls :)

As a sign of my devout relation to Allah, I built some of Baghdad's most grand and opulent mosques. Under my "faith campaign," I built training centers for Imams and instructed them to make a copy of the Koran written with my own blood.

Unfortunately, by the time we got halfway through the table of contents, I'd fainted twice, so we went for the KoliffNotes version. You can pick up a copy on Amazon...

Here is an excerpt:

Koran 002.195

...Do good; for Allah loveth those who do good.

And what if you do "no good." Like, for instance, a no-good villager intent on assassination. And his friends, and his friends' friends' cousins and their neighbors' daughters would also be no good. Well then Allah can not loveth them. I guess he hateth them, doesn't he? And if Allah hates them and they should accidentally have their intestines removed through their nostrils...well that's just too bad.

Koran 060.007

It may be that Allah will grant love and friendship between you and those whom ye now hold as enemies. For Allah has power over all things, and Allah is Oft-Forgiving, Most Merciful.

Are you kidding me? Fuck that.

Koran 002.190

...begin not hostilities. Lo! Allah loveth not aggressors.

You know, Allah loveth not aggressors. So if someone invades your country what are ya goin'a do? Hugh? What are ya goin'a do? Or let's say somebody with a couple hundred years of history under his belt steps into your kingdom that is thousands and thousands of years in the making? You gonna take that? I don't think so. Call out his mother first thing, then sucker punch the bitch while he's not looking. – BAM!!!

That's whatcha do!

Koran 002.060

Those who believe in the Koran, and those who follow The Jewish scriptures, and the Christians and the Sabians - any who believe in Allah and the Last Day, and work righteousness, shall have their reward with their Lord; on them shall be no fear, nor shall they grieve.

As long as Israel is destroyed in the process.

Koran 002.110

...be steadfast in prayer and regular in charity; And whatever good ye send forth for your souls before you, ye shall find it with Allah.

Scud missiles work well as a delivery system for that.

Koran 098.005

And they have been commanded no more than this: To worship Allah, offering Him sincere devotion, being true in faith; to establish regular prayer; and to practice regular charity; and that is the Religion Right and Straight.

Prayer has worked out well for me. I could order a merciless attack on Shiite rebels Wednesday afternoon, snort a line of coke off my girlfriend's chest at the club that night, drink a beer for breakfast, tell my second wife to kiss off, take in a torture at Abu Ghraib for lunch, get a hooker for Uday on Thursday night, and as long as I did my daily prayers, by the time Sabbath rolled around Friday morning, everything was cool.

Charity's another thing altogether. If it's not houses for Palestinian suicide bombers, I'm not interested.

Koran 103.002

Verily man is in loss, except such as have Faith, and do Righteous deeds, and join together In the mutual Teaching of Truth, and of Patience and Constancy.

It helps to have a lot of cash too.

Koran 002.205

Allah loveth not mischief.

Unless it's my half brother Ibrahim Barazan. That guy kills, literally. Totally cracks me up.

Koran 002.224

And make not Allah's name an excuse in your oaths against doing good, or acting rightly, or making peace between persons.

Fuck that too.

STRENGTH IS POWER

POSTED BY: SADDAM H.   AT 12:13 AM   (20) COMMENTS   PERMALINK ✉

comments

Like your half brother, Ibrahim, I too have had trouble with mischief. As a boy, mischief gave me great pleasure. I remember placing a scorpion down the Underoos of my first cousin and watching him squirm and laughing with delight.

I never lost this spirit. By Allah's name I shall not continue my mischievous behavior.

Posted by: AbdulPranksALot

Mr. Hussein,

We like your stuff. If you can only increase the arrogance level just a smidge to match our writing tone, we'll be happy to take some submissions for possible publication.

Writing in your own blood is a nice touch.

Posted by: mcsweeny's_editorial_dept

view more comments

Character Witnesses

Daily Trial Entry:

I am who I am, a simple farm boy who tried to make his country great. It is a matter of pride, and I am not an apologist. Because there are many people who will say that sort of thing for me, I have prepared a list of character witnesses that I will soon call to the stand...

The Dixie Chicks

Al Franken

Care Bears

Tim Robbins

Harry Belafonte

Cindy Sheehan

Susan Sarandon

The NY Times

Ted Kennedy

Howard Dean

Tinky Winky (not the other Teletubbies; they are evil)

Alec Baldwin

Sean Penn

Cast of *Boston Legal* (should come in character!)

Neil Young

Christopher Robin

Pink

Anyone From Canada

Mr. Frodo and Mr. Bilbo

The letter "V"

STRENGTH IS POWER

POSTED BY: SADDAM H.   AT 6:05 AM   (74) COMMENTS   PERMALINK ✉

Hey why isn't my name on your list? Didn't you see *Syriana*? Come on! I paid for that with my own money, well, at least produced it ... well, partnered in the production. Whatever. The point is, I should be on your list.

What about *Good Night and Good Luck*? That should count for something, too.

Posted by: TheCloonster

Character? You have no character. You are acting like the YIPPIE and other New Left defendants in the 60s and 70s and Ramsey Clark is on your defense team, too. Could there possibly be some little connection?

Posted by: Libertimothy

To Libertimothy: Yeah, no character. He should be made to shut up.

Posted by: NoSpin_Bill

This is the sort of thing that happens when the Romanian solution to a dictator problem isn't implemented. I got your witness right here.

Posted by: democracysong

The first step to showing that you are truly on a path to rehabilitation and/or reform is to address your shortcomings. This will, no doubt, also go a long way toward showcasing your character.

Take a deep breath and say with me: I tortured, maimed, raped, gassed, mutilated and murdered tens of thousands of my own citizens... Ok, good... now take another deep breath...

You know, it's just sickening how any educated person could want to execute another human being, especially someone like you that has so much to offer. Once rehabilitated, with your skill sets, you could start a new life, perhaps even in America – maybe move into a gated community and become the president of the Home Owners Association.

In fact, I know of one right now in Sherman Oaks. They are bickering all of the time and could use someone who will take control. You could make sure everyone picks up their dog poop, that no kids ride their skateboards on the walkway; you could even settle vicious land disputes between homeowners.

You could become an assistant high school principal. All a teacher would have to say is, "Do you want to go down to Mr. Hussein's office?" These are talents that only a unique individual such as yourself possesses but they're going to put you to death. Why? Why?

Posted by: justice_angel

Shut up.

Posted by: NoSpin_Bill

Seriously, I should be on your list.

Posted by: TheCloonster

To Libertimothy: I agree with democracysong. If he doesn't behave, what about chaining him to the chair with a gag over his big mouth?

You know, duct tape is good for just about any leakage...

Posted by: ViagraPatriot

You should put Bu$h on the stand. It will be amusing to watch him start changing his tune, keeping in mind that the quality most essential to working in the Bu$h White House is the ability to lie.

Posted by: LarryCurlyandJezass

Shut up. Shut up. Shut up. SHUT UP!

Posted by: NoSpin_Bill

---

view more comments

Why I Invade My Neighbors

Daily Trial Entry:

I keep hearing, "Saddam killed my family, Saddam tortured my uncle, Saddam buried my village in a cloud of nerve gas, wah, wah, etc., etc." This is very unfair. So much is taken out of context. These uncles, and children, and villagers, or whatever were all guilty of something! Spying for our enemies, trying to assassinate me, going past-due on their cable. I had good reason! I was doing this for the good of the people. Well, not the good of the people in these particular villages, but you get my meaning.

In my defense, I must include this explanation: As the reincarnation of Nebuchadnezzar, ruler of Babylon and king of Mesopotamia and the lands of the central Islamic states, my plan was to unite the peoples of the region as one Pan-Arab nation. Therefore, it was necessary to do what any *"president"* of Iraq might have to undertake to secure *"his"* state.

But geopolitics is a complicated business, and it is difficult for people to have it wrapped about their heads. It is possible this has been lost on people who think the Middle East is somewhere between Boston and Wilmington.

While I was in court today I made a few sketches to help explain. First here's the world:

Evil Pacmen devouring everything...Waka Waka Waka...Make it stop! Please! I no longer wish to be a cherry.

And here is a map of the Babylonian Empire, the rightful lands of the Arab. Persians have laid claim to it, but they are bastards with bad breath. Iraq? Iran? Syria? Israel? Palestine? All countries that the British made up after WWI or II or something, anyway. They are bastards with bad breath *and* bad teeth.

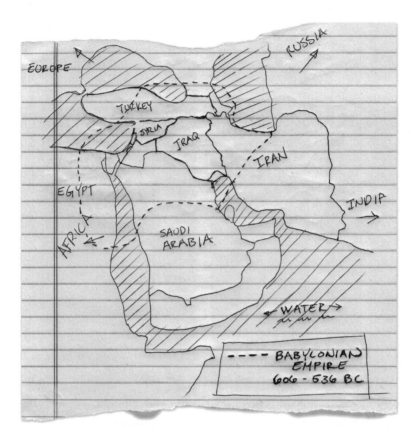

— *BTW ... Mesopotamia means the land between two rivers (the Tigris and Euphrates). Known as the birthplace of civilization whose capital was the city of Babylon (very close to Baghdad, makes for an easy commute).*

Now take Iran and Kuwait – PLEASE ;-)

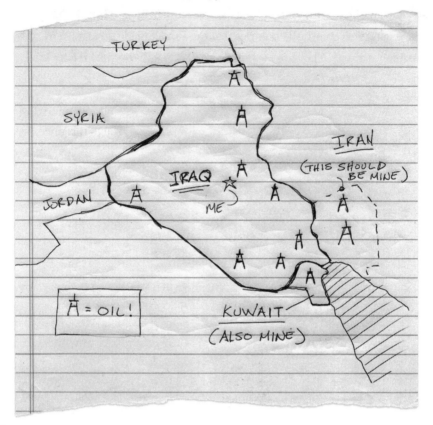

The Iran War was an obvious must. Iran is just one letter away from Iraq. It was too tempting. So easy I couldn't resist. If Canada was called the United States of Americo, believe me one of your presidents would have tried to grab it. Your Teddy Roosevelt or Andrew Jackson, or James Polk would have tried. Why should I be any different?

Why did I invade Kuwait? 'Cause it sounds like a fruit, and it's an oddly shaped country. Frankly, it is in the way of Iraq. In America, you called it "manifest destiny." We call it "ours."

It's really that simple.

It is possible I've been a bit greedy though, wanting to reunite the Pan-Arab nations under the banner of all of Babylon. In the future I'll offer to make adjustments to my plan. Maybe this will work:

- In the north, I'll let the Kurds go back to being Turks or whatever the hell they want to call themselves these days.

- It's important the Persians (you know them as Iranians) make a concession to lasting peace and let the *"disputed"* territories come home to the Arabs (me). But I'll let the rest of the country alone – promise.

- It goes without saying that Kuwait is part of Babylon, and therefore has always been a province of Iraq. Please we've been through this once.

– This is going to go over big in court. Must remember to show these to Ramsey, my American lawyer, to see if he "gets it."

Finally, with a small nudge of a province here, a little tug of a border there, we arrive at a very nice map of the new Iraq, which I think would be nice to call:

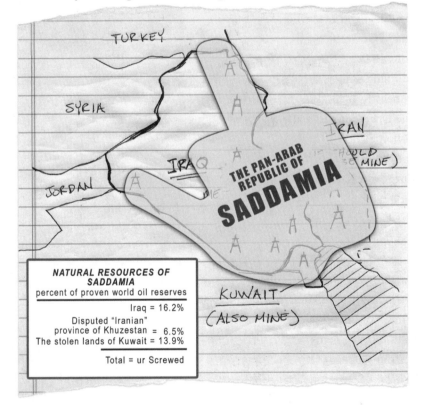

– I should remember to call Kinkos to see about getting this enlarged and placed on poster-board.

STRENGTH IS POWER

The People Who Did It

Daily Trial Entry:

I know I did not commit crimes against humanity. I must be released immediately so that I may find the real killers! Every day that goes by is another day that these satanic devils will use to destroy evidence and disappear into the general public. If the Americans are not willing to go after these murderous thugs then it is up to me alone to find them.

I pledge this to the Iraqi people; if set free, I will commit every waking minute of my life to finding the people responsible for this carnage. I will not sleep until each and every one of them is brought to justice. I have compiled a list of potential suspects to these heinous crimes:

My estranged first wife
Simon Cowell
Tony Blair
O.J. Simpson
Donald Rumsfeld
The Orkin man (it's always the quiet ones you least suspect)
Robert Blake
Pat Robertson
Hurricane Katrina
Exxon-Mobil
The One-armed man
Judith Miller
Sharon Stone's vagina
An angry and Vengeful Allah
The butler in the kitchen with the candlestick
Stone Cold Steve Austin
Bill Clinton's penis
Chucky Cheese
Sharks
Itchy and Scratchy
Barney

STRENGTH IS POWER

POSTED BY: SADDAM H.   AT 7:17 PM   (238) COMMENTS   PERMALINK ✉

Hey, Hey, Hey! I may be a heartless critic of the weak-willed and the pathetic. It is true that I take great pleasure in seeing worthless, talentless worms writhe in agony as I crush their most cherished dreams with soul wrenching disdain – But crimes against humanity? You got the wrong guy on that one.

Posted by: Idol_Simon

Saddam Hussein is innocent of all crime. Saddam is a most wonderful man. I am the owner of a farm with lots of spider holes and Saddam stayed in one of them for a while. He was an excellent tenant. I never heard him complain once, occasionally I would hear a shriek or two but no more.

He minded his own business, didn't bring any type of pets with him. I hate pets they can ruin a good spider hole in one day. He always emptied his defecation bucket each day. He paid on time and far more than the rental fee – a handful of uncut diamonds each month. He is a very generous man – although I must say it is one of my finest spider holes on the whole property: concrete slab sitting area, real air holes, and hand packed mud walls.

He only asked for one thing during his stay, if I could get him a one way ticket to French Guiana. I could not help him. I do not know what is a French Guiana but I brought him a French pastry and he was very happy. That was it. Not one complaint. He was a perfect gentleman.

Posted by: S_Holes4Rent

As I repetitively said, I can't fault any of those Americans who still believe in the lies their President still repeats. I blame the media responsible for brainwashing them. Again it's the biased, mainsteam media that tends to serve the world superpower leaders at the expense of poor nations devastated by those leaders' arrogant policies, and political agendas.

The media has done it. Put them on your list.

Posted by: Yuhud69

I am telling you right now to shut your pie hole.

Posted by: NoSpin_Bill

Could I at least be on this list then?

Posted by: TheCloonster

I think they should put a digital voice box on you that will make your voice sound like Donald Duck. LOL

Posted by: RangerRed

To RangerRed: That is a childish comment. We are talking about genocide and possibly hanging a man here.

Posted by: BlueBob

To BlueBob: quack, quack, I'm Schadadam Huschsein tsmmmmd, quack

Posted by: RangerRed

To RangerRed: I have an advanced degree in sociology and I logged onto SaddamDump to post a few comments and do some research into what makes this man tick and his larger role in the world hegemony. I expected to find rousing or even brusque debate but quack, quack is hardly engaging.

Posted by: BlueBob

To BlueBob: queer.

Posted by: RangerRed

To RangerRed: sh*t kicker

Posted by: BlueBob

To BlueBob: homo.

Posted by: RangerRed

To RangerRed: illetarate inbred

Posted by: BlueBob

To BlueBob: I believe the correct spelling is **illiterate** inbred.

Posted by: RangerRed

To RangerRed: fag

Posted by: BlueBob

view more comments

THE SADDAM DUMP

[Why I Did It]

Who's Laughing Now?

Daily Trial Entry:

Today there are many reports about the conduct of the newly-appointed judge in my case. Here are a few of the headlines about what happened:

. . . .

Hussein Trial Erupts, and Expulsions Ensue
– NY Times

Hussein's Day at Trial: More Rancor and a Fight
Pandemonium Greets New Chief Judge, Who Orders Ex-Leader Removed From Courtroom
– Washington Post

More Chaos At Saddam Trial
– CBS News

. . . .

Chaos! Rancor! Expulsions! Pandemonium! – *Bah!* None told of the events accurately. The press is biased. They all want to make me as a joke butt. But I am no joke butt, for the court is a butt and not me! Especially the new judge– *he is ridiculous*. And so for the record to be straightened, this is how I would have reported what happened...

The uproar began moments after the new judge, Raouf Abdel-Rahman, took his seat at the bench. He didn't realize there was a whoopee cushion there, *(tee hee)* and he made the farting noise.

After the laughter calmed, the judge announced that he would not allow his courtroom to be used by the defendants to make "political speeches, or the farting noises."

When my half-brother, Barzan Ibrahim, rose to complain, a yelling match erupted, punctuated repeatedly by Ibrahim's use of a brass horn strapped to his waist by a cord. The judge ordered Ibrahim to leave. To which Ibrahim replied, "This court is the daughter of a whore." – *honk, honk.*

Ibrahim was dragged from the courtroom by four guards as the six other defendants and their 13 lawyers, and I began dancing a jig, while singing, "Long live Iraq! Long live Iraq! This court is the daughter of a whore! Long Live Iraq! Long Live Iraq!"

"We've had enough of this! Sit down! Sit down!" yelled the judge, leaping to his feet.

The defense team then walked out in protest with their noses in the air.

The judge immediately appointed three new lawyers, who were waiting outside, apparently prepared for a ruckus. *(here's a picture)*

I then announced that I also wanted to leave, saying I refused to accept the authority of the new lawyers. "Can't you see they are stooges?" I yelled, which triggered another heated exchange with the judge.

"I ask you to permit me to leave because I can't bear to stay at least for this session, until these problems get solved," I said, wagging my finger.

"The court has decided to throw you out," the judge responded.

"Don't say I'm being thrown out!" I shouted furiously. "You are Iraqi, and Iraqis show respect for people who are older in age. I led you for 35 years, and now you say, 'Throw him out'? This is shameful of you."

"I am a judge, and you are a defendant. Shame on you," said the judge.

"No, shame on you."

"You."

"No, you."

"I'm rubber and you are glue, whatever you say bounces off me and sticks to you."

"I decided by myself to leave," I insisted. "Don't say I'm being thrown out."

"Do you want to leave? You are being thrown out!" countered the judge.

Glancing scornfully around the room, I then strode out…

At this, the judge gave a huff and sat heavily onto the whoopee cushion … again (*ha ha*).

He had no choice but to clear the courtroom and call another recess, due to excessive giggling.

Now, does that sound like a joke butt to you?

— *Just a thought, I might want to go back to the mustache look and add a big cigar this time.*

STRENGTH IS POWER

POSTED BY: SADDAM H.   AT 12:48 PM   (14) COMMENTS   PERMALINK ✉

Saddam, you never cease to amaze me. Been a fan for a long time. Started watching you back in the seventies when you marched all of your uncle's cabinet members out of Parliament and shot them one after the other.

Great daytime television!

This latest thing with the judge and the court proves that you are one of the great entertainers of our time – really funny stuff.

Keep up the shtick.

Posted by: watching_headsroll

I am the new president of CBS news. I want to tell you that we make every effort to cover the news in general, and your trial specifically, with the utmost objectivity and unbiased journalistic integrity.

Oh sure, people deride us for the national guard story we ran on 60 Minutes about G.W. playing "hooky." And Dan Rather is the poster boy for the East-coast liberal media elite. But you know what pal? Here's a news flash — You are guilty, and that's what we'll be reporting, end of story. Because that's the way the news is run now that FOX has upped the ante: "Form an opinion, find evidence to support it, and then report it as fact." Or haven't you ever heard of "truthiness"?
BTW – We knew you were trying to be funny. Your act just wasn't cutting it – sorry. If you can't take a bad review now and again, get out of the business.

Posted by: McManus_matters

Dude,

Here's some stuff that might help make your act more current. I mean, come on ... the Marx Brothers? How old are they? Like they must be in their fifties already, right?

So yeah here ya go ... You should scream into the mic and roll around on the floor, and kind of make weird body gestures that are sexually suggestive. Also, curse more. This will make your audience freak out a little, but they'll think you're being edgy. It works really well for me.

Posted by: Dane_Cook29

view more comments

Israel Is The Problem

Note To Self:

Israel must be destroyed. Israel is to blame for most of our problems, my Arab brothers. It is Israel that keeps most of the Arab people in sand when they mock us with trees. It is Israel that allows such scorching summer heat in our lands. It is Israel that keeps us wrapped in sheets when they wear modern western clothes. It is Israel that doesn't allow a decent standard of living in our Arab countries no matter how much oil we pump. It is Israel that makes Arab people appear darker than they actually are. It is Israel that builds a large fence and imprisons all Arabs in their own countries. It is Israel that keeps the great Arab moviemakers suppressed. It is Israel that keeps Arabs from landing on the moon. It is Israel that keeps Omar Sharif from winning an Oscar. It is Israel that doesn't allow Budweiser to use Arabian Horses instead of those lumbering Clydesdales. It is Israel that keeps me from getting a good Jew lawyer. We must destroy it, my Arab brothers before we melt.

– How can I work this into defense? Closing arguments? Impromptu speech? Perhaps during a faked epileptic seizure? Must keep from Ramsey, he'll water it down too much (such a pussy!). Perhaps Omar Sharif could make an appearance on my behalf?!!

STRENGTH IS POWER

POSTED BY: SADDAM H.   AT 4:47 AM   (91) COMMENTS   PERMALINK ✉

comments

I want to raise a finger here Mr. Hussein. Israel is not to blame for the mess you Arabs have created. You know, I was at a friend's home yesterday (very wealthy and well-educated so they know a thing or two about a thing or two) and we were all in agreement on this. Those Palestinian terrorists cause all of the trouble over there. Awful people, filthy actually, even there own kind don't want them. They should just stay on their side of the wall – and blow each other up.

Posted by: Miriam_K

---

view more comments

I Take The Cake

Daily Trial Entry:

Soooooo... Here we are. This is tiresome, but I must. Ladies and gentlemen, the envelope please; in the category of crimes against humanity filed but not yet prosecuted are:

. . . .

Charges Facing Saddam Hussein
– BBC

The preliminary charges relate to the following:

• **Anfal 'ethnic cleansing' campaign against Kurds, 1988**
...Saddam Hussein ordered a massive displacement operation of the Kurdish population in northern Iraq.

• **Gassing Kurds in Halabja in 1988**
...Iraqi forces attacked the Kurdish town of Halabja with bombs containing a mixture of mustard and nerve gases. An estimated 5,000 civilians, including women, children and babies, were killed in a single day. Gen. Ali Hassan al-Majid ordered the attack, earning the notorious epithet "Chemical Ali."

• **Invasion of Kuwait, 1990**
...Iraqi soldiers are alleged to have tortured and summarily executed prisoners and to have looted Kuwait City and taken hundreds of Kuwaiti captives back to Baghdad. Iraqi soldiers also set fire to more than 700 oil wells and opened pipelines to let oil pour into the Gulf and other water sources.

• **Crushing the Kurdish and Shia rebellions after the 1991 Gulf War**
...The Iraqi army suppressed the uprisings using massive military force and drained the southern marsh lands which had sustained a way of life dating back around 5,000 years.

• **Killing political activists over 30 years**
Evidence has emerged of 270 mass graves across Iraq which are believed to hold the remains of possibly tens of thousands of people. The UN Commission on Human Rights condemned the Iraqi regime in 2001 for "widespread, systematic torture.

• **Massacre of members of the Kurdish Barzani tribe in 1983**
...Iraqi security forces arrested about 8,000 male members of the Barzani clan in the northern province of Arbil. They were transported to southern Iraq and have not been heard of since.

46

- **Killing of religious leaders in 1974**
  ...the Iraqi regime arrested dozens of Shia religious leaders, and executed five of them.
. . . .

I spit the raspberry at these charges. *Blthhhhhhh!* These crimes against humanity seem like a mere parking violation when you consider how long I've been in power. I have been President of Iraq for 35 years.

That is a lot of elections.

Imagine how many people George Bush would have had to kill to stay in power for 35 years. Half of America would be dead: the entire Democratic Party, CNN, NY Times, ACLU, all American university professors, all the Jews, Muslims, Dick Cheney's daughter, every member of the Screen Actors Guild, Greenpeace and the Sierra Club members, teachers, lawyers, Hybrid owners, all employees of National Lampoon, and anyone named Josh.

When you think about it, these charges are relatively insignificant. As President of an Arab country filled with Jihadists, oil rich separatists, and many tribal divisions, you would think I would have killed millions by now. I think I'm only in the thousands. That's not that bad.

Hitler was responsible for killing over 30 million people, Stalin 40 million, Mau Tse Tung 38 million. So what's all the fuss? If we go by the numbers, I rank somewhere between benevolent and gracious.

— *I deserve a Nobel Peace Prize.*

Americans had Vietnam, the Cold War, Bay of Pigs, the War in Iraq, another War in Iraq, the War on Poverty, the War on Drugs, the War on Terror, and Oliver North, and they're winning peace prizes all of the time!

— *So why not me?*

I kept a country of fanatical, fractious, frenetic freaks from exploding into a civil war for almost 4 decades. Now that's what I call an example of peaceful leadership. I am Saddam Hussein, Middle East peacemaker; give me the Nobel Peace Prize.

— *I deserve what I get!*

STRENGTH IS POWER

POSTED BY: SADDAM H.   AT 6:00 PM   (82) COMMENTS   **PERMALINK** ✉

comments

Under direct orders I hid a small vial containing Bubonic Plague in my rectum. I am still scared to remove it even though I have not had a proper bowel movement in two years. Please advise immediately. I might explode, causing thousands of needless deaths.

Posted by: ButtPlague

The Nobel Prize should be given to you. The world will seldom see another peacemaker such as you Saddam. I know because I too am a peaceable man. I remember when I was a boy and my father, the "great leader," would say to me, "Kim Jong, the peaceful fox acts like a lunatic in winter but builds nuclear weapons in springtime."

If you had obtained the nuclear arsenal that you deserved, the peace that you could have created would be almost as great as the peace that I am making now.

BTW I have happy disco shoe too.

Posted by: DearLeader

---

view more comments

I Can't Believe I Ate The Whole Thing

Note To Self:

As I try to build a case for my character there are times when I am frustrated. There are peoples in this world who do not know how to be grateful. It is such a simple thing to receive the blessings of a benevolent leader and to make homage and supplication in return. But some have a hard time expressing it. Here is an email from that kind of person:

> Hi,
>
> Saddam, I was your food tester for 8 and a half years. If you remember, I came down with botulism, E-coli, bubonic plague, hepatitis B, C, H, rheumatic fever, rickets, 24-hour stomach flu, chronic hiccups, uncontrollable projectile vomiting, and the measles (very dangerous to get as an adult).
>
> The doctors say my intestines are worn out, and my stomach lining is almost completely gone. But yet, I am not mentioned in the crimes against humanity trial. It is as if my suffering does not count.
>
> Why?

What gibberish! This was his job! He agreed to do this and was paid handsomely. He was given the Republican Guard Gold Crescent for Valor, and received major medical for life – no one gets major medical – not even most Americans. And now he is complaining? I personally gave him my blood during two blood transfusions, and would have given him my kidney if we were a match. He is a despicable, ungrateful little man.

I wonder if he would enjoy his food more without a nose.

STRENGTH IS POWER

POSTED BY: SADDAM H.   AT 8:44 PM   (39) COMMENTS   PERMALINK ✉

Could you hit me back with your food testers contact info? Mine's been calling in sick a lot lately.

Posted by: Number43

I am President of the International Food Testers Union. IFTU is a small group of loyal workers who provide a unique trade to over 35 tyrannical despots around the world. As a member of IFTU you'll have the advantage of the finest union leadership fighting for the best wages and benefits.

You'll also receive our award winning monthly newsletter: "What's That Smell," featuring articles like: "You Don't Have to Eat That," "How to Avoid Vomiting at All Cost," "Beating Botulism," "Keeping Perfect Absenteeism," and "The Morning Pick-Me-Up."

IFTU union dues are not cheap but well worth it. 97 percent of our fees go to our health plan the rest go to burial expenses. It's a wonderful opportunity for anybody who wants to get into the food-testing field. See us on the web at: www.InternationalFoodTestersUnion.org

Posted by: IFTUrockshard

Hey what kind of rifle is that you're always waving around? You know, the one that you shoot in the air in front of large crowds. No one ever seems to get hit and you shoot it everywhere! I'd like to give that model a try.

Posted by: DeadeyeDick

Your food tester is complaining? I was made to start all of your cars before you got in. I am now just a head living somewhere in Ethiopia. At least he has limbs.

Posted by: JustA_Head

view more comments

To Coup Or Not To Coup

Daily Trial Entry:

I'm not really doing much today. There's been another recess, and I'm bored. My lawyers seem to think prolonging things is in my best interest – whatever.

As I'm writing this, I see that there is a fresh rotation of young Americans to keep guard of me. They are all nice young men. I like them very much; they are very polite, and they seem to like my poetry and laugh at my jokes.

They are from different places, with strange names like Akron, and Duluth. Why name a place that way? Halabja – now there is a proper name for a place, but no matter, still nice to have them here. They all have similar interests to young men anywhere. Reminds me of when my boys were their age.

They treat me as their grandfather and ask me many questions. I expect these new boys will be the same. Here is how I imagine our conversation may go…

Guard: So Mr. Hussein, you seem to be a very hip and stylish dude for your age. You talk about the ladies like you're a real stud. How can I too be like you, and do the hook up with the young jezebel?

Me: Do not fret my young guard son there is a way for you to attract the ladies. Here is the checklist to follow:

1) Grow a moustache
2) Wear a military uniform at all times…
3) Obtain some oil fields.
4) And carry out a top-level political assassination

I very much relate to your personal yearnings. As you can see it is difficult for me to have relations with a young lady here. But for you, by following these simple rules you will get a hook up any time you want.

Guard: Thank you sir. That is very helpful. I was wondering. When I get back home, I'm definitely not going to sign up to come back here and fight this horrible, horrible war that my lying president got me into. So I will require a new employment. Do you have advice for me to find the new job?

Me: Finding a good employment is the best thing for a young man as yourself. It will start you on a path to wealth and happiness. Here is the checklist to follow:

> 1) Grow a moustache
>
> 2) Wear a military uniform at all times...
>
> 3) Obtain some oil fields.
>
> 4) And carry out a top-level political assassination

This will insure that you obtain not only a good employment, but also a country you can truly call your own. By following these simple rules, you will be able to have wealth and power and the authority to kill people you do not like.

Guard: Wow, that makes a lot of sense, Saddam. Listen, this may seem a bit odd, but I have been wishing to purchase an automobile that really makes the pimping. Can you tell me how to acquire such a thing?

Me: It is fortunate that you ask me this. There are many things to ponder when purchasing an automobile: sticker price vs. drive off value, mpg vs. performance and handling, whether 14 percent interest on a used car will put my monthly payment outside the cost value ratio of buying new over the life of the car. Here is the checklist to follow:

> 1) Grow a moustache
>
> 2) Wear a military uniform at all times...
>
> 3) Obtain some oil fields.
>
> 4) And carry out a top-level political assassination

In a very short period of time, you will be chauffeured everywhere in an all black stretch limousine with tinted bulletproof windows, armor plating, and little flags on the hood. — Enjoy!

STRENGTH IS POWER

POSTED BY: SADDAM H.   AT 7:23 AM   (22) COMMENTS   **PERMALINK** ✉

I have had the pleasure of guarding Saddam since he's been put on trial. He's like your grandfather, always with a story, and very good advice on things, like with back home stuff.

Last week, I got word from my wife that our house was going into foreclosure – I haven't worked in my real job since late 2002 – Saddam was outraged and called the mortgage company with my cell phone. He got them to eliminate all interest on the loan and give me a 6-month grace payment period – he was amazing. It was so effortless for him; he got the mortgage lady to reveal her immediate family's names, and then slipped into the conversation something about "Iraqi sleeper cells operating in the U.S." – she just caved — it was incredible!

Yeah, it was all a bunch of talk, but that's what Saddam does.

Posted by: SeenSaddamDumping

I am Colonel Wadesworth, US Army 2nd Brigade. Okay this is it. We mean it. We can get you out of there now! I have an entire Army battalion willing to walk you out of that prison and right back to your presidential palace.

This has to happen soon. I just had an entire squadron blow up while building a preschool. Then a few of my military ambulances took the wounded to the hospital and they were blown up. Five soldiers started carrying the injured from that blast on their backs but then they were blown up. Finally the only remaining survivor, a 3-year-old boy with no arms or legs, managed to roll himself down a small hill to the emergency room. He's fine.

The next time you're on the courtroom cameras wave to us as a signal that you are prepared to go forward.

Posted by: ColonelWade

---

view more comments

Express Yourself

Daily Trial Entry:

Yesterday, in the trial Barzan made a prank and I learned a valuable lesson.
Here is part of the story:

. . . .

Saddam Hussein's Former Intelligence Chief (Barzan Ibrahim), Wearing Pajamas In Court As A Protest.

...Ibrahim complained that he and other defendants had been forced to attend the proceedings against their will.

"You brought me by force in my pajamas and I have been on a hunger strike for two days," he said. "Are you familiar with the law, or did they just bring you here?" Ibrahim asked Abdel-Rahman provocatively. The judge ignored the questions and smiled.

Juhi, commenting on Ibrahim's attire, told reporters: "You must have noticed that all the defendants wore appropriate attire. Defendant Barzan (Ibrahim) wore what he thought was appropriate."...

... also displayed to the court a document dated July 21, 1982 — 13 days after the assassination attempt — in which the Mukhabarat, the intelligence agency headed by Ibrahim at the time, recommended rewards for six employees for their role in the arrests.

The document bore a signature that the prosecution said was Ibrahim's. Below it was written the word "agreed" with what was allegedly Saddam's signature.

On the witness stand, Hamed Youssef Hamadi — Saddam's secretary at the time — was asked whose handwriting was on the memo. "It looks like President Saddam's," he said.

Ibrahim disputed the authenticity of the document. He cross-examined all three witnesses and at the same time gave his own account of his role in the Dujail crackdown. Abdel-Rahman allowed him to speak, largely uninterrupted.
– *Associated Press*

. . . .

My half-brother Barzan is a real joker, isn't he? Always coming up with the new ways to make me laugh. Like that time he pretended he was dancing with a young Kurdish girl after dismembering her family and stabbing her 37 times in the chest. He calls to me and says, "Hey Dammy know who we are?

Fred Astaire and Ginger 'oh god no! Please no! Agh gah gah no blub blub blub'." Ho, Ho that guy is a hoot.

BTW it's o.k. — They were Iranian spies. Should have seen what he did with the other bodies… ROTFL

Anyway, this morning we knew the guards would force us to come to court against our will. So, when they came for us, I knew he might pull something. As they approached, he whispers to me, "Hey Dammy, I'm going to court in my underwear today." I almost made the urine in my trousers. It was so funny.

You know he got a lot of attention. He probably was able to say, "lying dog Bush," and "I am wrongly accused" about ten or fifteen times more than he usually does. People just don't know what to say to a man standing in a court of law defending himself against charges of mass murder, crimes against humanity, and genocide – while wearing nothing but a pair of long johns.

You have to admit that's funny.

This has made me think. Perhaps I may learn from Barzan's antics. I need to be lightened up. Have more fun and express myself with more pizzazz. My friend Chirac is always saying "*Joie de Vivre*, Saddam, *Joie de Vivre.*" But who knows what he's saying – fucking French.

In any case, what I have learned from this experience is, "Express yourself through the clothes that you wear." This is especially important for the children to learn. So I have prepared a bit of something for them…

COSTUMING FOR THE IRAQI COURT
A fun exercise for kids of all ages!

Illustration A – Saddam doll

Step 1: Start by printing out the Saddam paper doll in Illustration A. Glue the printout to a piece of thin cardboard for support and then trim around the doll with scissors. Don't forget to do the same for the stand "Illustration B." You don't want Saddam to fall on his face!

Illustration B – Stand

Step 2: Print out your favorite costume from the following illustrations.

Step 3: Cut out the costume with scissors.

Step 4: Use the tabs to secure the costume to your Saddam paper doll.

Educational suggestions are printed under each illustration to make "play time" a "learning time" as well.

Illustration C – The Statesman With Rifle

The Statesman outfit is perfect for looking regal and legal. This is very important for showing up in court, to look proper so the judge can see that you are honest and dignified. The rifle is a nice touch for your first day in court, because nothing says "dignified" and "in charge" more than a dark grey suit, white shirt, fedora, and a .385 Remington Magnum. Skipping the tie is also a nice flare – thanks Tom Cruise.

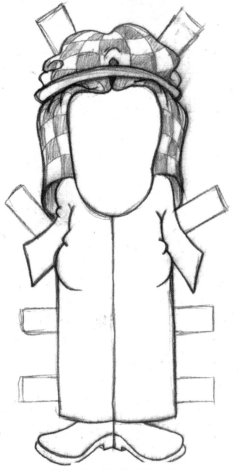

Illustration D – The Bedouin

The Bedouin outfit is a nod to the locals. Personally I think it makes me look like Homer Simpson in a muumuu, but it does keep me tight with my Arab brothers and it's good for days when all your boxers are in the laundry (if you know what I mean).

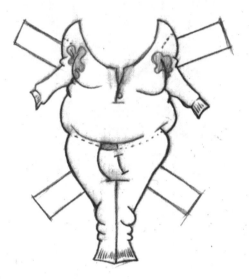

Illustration E – Long Johns

The Long John outfit works well to confuse everyone around you who might try to take you or anything else seriously. The more you yell and scream and pretend to say important things, the funnier it gets. Your friends won't be able to keep a straight face. Big ups to Barzan.

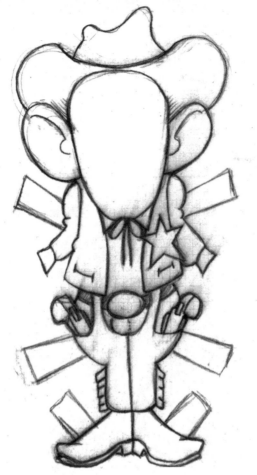

Illustration F – The Sheriff's In Town

The Sheriff's In Town outfit works best for intimidation, making unjustified accusations, rash decisions, and the ladies love the big ears.

When wearing this outfit, don't take "no" for an answer, or "yes," or "maybe" either. As a matter of fact, don't bother with asking…
you already know.

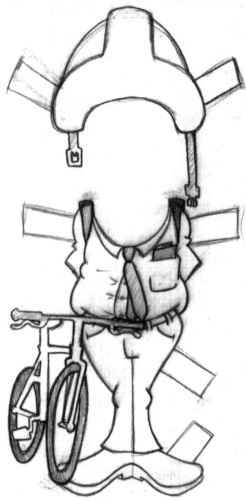

Illustration G – The Mormon Missionary

The Mormon Missionary outfit is the perfect costume to wear on days that you just feel like listening to the sound of your own voice. You can talk, and talk, and talk, and talk.

This set of clothing and convenient hip-attached bicycle have special numbing powers, rendering your audience helpless to the torrent of words that will undoubtedly flow from your gaping maw.

If you're losing the case, wear this. It's an excellent delaying tactic unto itself.

Illustration H – The Janitor

The Janitor outfit is specifically designed to blend into any crowd.

It has cloaking capability that leaves you invisible in groupings of two or more. Trust me, no one will even glance in your direction when you are wearing this outfit.

This of course, is a selection best used as a last resort. Put it on and slip out the side door with the bang of the gavel.
Good luck.

STRENGTH IS POWER

Hey a**hole, you forgot a costume. You should have one with a rope around your neck and a hood on your head!

Posted by: UpUrz

My daughter and I tried your exercise together during creative time this afternoon. Her playdate's mom and I really enjoyed coloring, cutting, and pasting the parts together for the girls. Sally and her friend spent most of the afternoon watching TV so I'm not sure how much they learned, but us moms are way educated about the Iraqi court and what to wear now.

BTW UR cute.

Posted by: SuzyCluz

Here's an expression for you:

You get to mouth off on this blog about anything you want. You have a blog, a cell phone, television, hmmm? – all American inventions. You Arabs are always trash-talking America but it's Americans that gave you half the crap you use to spew your hatred.

Stop using the American created blog and Internet too.

Posted by: ReaganLuvr

I had so much fun with the sheriff costume!!! I made an extra doll and dressed him as the little statesman feller and then the sheriff says, "reach for the sky" but he couldn't 'cause he's just a little paper doll, see. So the sheriff shot him Bang, Bang. This is the most fun I've had since I turned sober.

Can you do one of "the decider?" Not sure what that looks like. Maybe it's a cross between the Hulk and Crusader-X.

Posted by: Number43

Would you like to take a personality test?

Posted by: Suri_Cruise

view more comments

THE SADDAM DUMP

[I Bomb Your Freedom]

I Bomb Your Freedom

Thoughts:

Now that George W. admits he will never find the WMDs, he says that his unprovoked invasion is about giving the Iraqi people freedom. You Americans, with all your freedoms. Everything is about freedom! Nobody is free! When I lived in the palace, I wasn't free, because I was a celebrity, because I would be mobbed! You wouldn't expect to see Tom Cruise at Ralphs would you? – Same with me. When the people love you, it is a blessing, but you are not free.

I could not go anywhere, and I am President! I couldn't walk through shopping malls and purchase one of those Sharper Image Massage Chairs anytime I wanted to. I couldn't even go to a movie and shout, "I will kill the Jew producer who made this piece of crap!" I couldn't go anywhere. Yet I was happy, very happy, as were my people.

My subjects had more freedom than me. They could walk anywhere they wanted (as long as it was in a government-approved sector.) They were allowed to speak openly in cafes about a variety of subjects: the weather and football scores. They could discuss science while in my underground laboratories, and even politics, during interrogation sessions.

They had freedom.

The Iraqi daily newspaper, run by my son Qusay, went out of its way to inform the Iraqi people. Too many newspapers can leave the people confused and unsure of their direction in life. By providing one newspaper, we freed the people from the clutter of too many different opinions so they could pursue the real things in life that matter.

Now *that* is freedom.

But this isn't enough for the American Imperialists. You think you must bring your brand of freedom to everybody. Well, I say, "I don't want your freedom."

The only freedom the Iraqi people want is freedom from America, freedom to kill each other the way we choose.

I bomb your freedom.

STRENGTH IS POWER

POSTED BY: SADDAM H.   AT 8:16 AM   (340) COMMENTS   PERMALINK ✉

comments

Everything is 'bomb this' and 'bomb that.' How many countries are we going to bomb into freedom? And how many people do the insurgents have to blow up before the world realizes that they are hurting inside?

Posted by: BlueBob

To BlueBob: If you ask me, that whole area over there is the problem. I've got 2 words: Glass Parkinglot. (That might be three words)

Posted by: RangerRed

To RangerRed: You're an idiot.

Posted by: BlueBob

To BlueBob: I bomb you.

Posted by: RangerRed

To RangerRed: That is hate speech. I hope the moderator kicks you off.

Posted by: BlueBob

To BlueBob: bomb, bomb, bomb, bomb, bomb, bomb, bomb, bomb, bomb, bomb.

Posted by: RangerRed

To RangerRed: Oh that's great, now we're both going to end up on a watch list. Smart move Einstein.

Posted by: BlueBob

view more comments

Hunger Strike!

Daily Trial Entry

I am holding a hunger strike protesting the Kurdish "Pigman" judge's treatment of me and my co-defendants. I shall go with no food until he and his American masters allow me to express my defense without being told to shut-up, sit down, stand in the corner, or write 1000 words on paper telling why I am not allowed to speak in the courtroom without being called on first. I shall not stand for such demeaning treatment ever again. Therefore, from this day I shall officially be without food. I choose not to eat.

My hunger strike begins.

STRENGTH IS POWER

POSTED BY: SADDAM H.   AT 9:45 PM   (0) COMMENTS   PERMALINK ⊠

comments

Day 1 Of Hunger Strike

I sit here waiting for my trial. Yes, I am hungry. My American guards taunt me. They eat those Nacho Cheese Doritos outside my cell. The smell of the Nacho Cheese fills my nose. One bite, and a man is in the jaws of his enemy. Praise be Allah that I can rid myself of this Satanic desire. May I have the strength of 12 oxen so that I can fight these Nacho Cheese Doritos.

STRENGTH IS POWER

POSTED BY: SADDAM H.   AT 11:46 PM   (0) COMMENTS   PERMALINK ⊠

comments

Day 2 Of Hunger Strike

Shit, I'm hungry!

STRENGTH IS POWER

POSTED BY: SADDAM H.   AT 12:05 AM   (0) COMMENTS   PERMALINK ✉

comments

Day 3 Of Hunger Strike

Americans are blowing in the smell of their fast food.

It's KFC ... fried chicken! Must resist!

STRENGTH IS POWER

POSTED BY: SADDAM H.   **AT 11:48 AM**   **(0) COMMENTS**   <u>**PERMALINK**</u> ✉

comments

Day 4 ... The Chips Are Back!

Americans throw into my cell an open bag of Nacho Cheese Doritos and an open canister of Pizza Pringles. Allah provide me the strength. Maybe I can have just one chip. Yes, I shall. One chip. It would still be a fast. One chip is not really breaking the hunger strike.

No one will ever know.

STRENGTH IS POWER

POSTED BY: SADDAM H.   AT 5:22 PM   (0) COMMENTS   PERMALINK ✉

comments

Day 5 ... I Am Weak

Ate an entire bag of Nacho Cheese Doritos... Pizza Pringles all gone.

STRENGTH IS POWER

POSTED BY: SADDAM H.   **AT** 2:41 AM   (0) **COMMENTS**   **PERMALINK** ✉

comments

Day 6

No man can resist the power of the McNugget. One dip in the open tub of hot mustard sauce, and I am no more. The Great Satan defeats me … I must stay strong.

The food will stop now!

STRENGTH IS POWER

POSTED BY: SADDAM H.   AT 1:02 PM   (0) COMMENTS   PERMALINK ✉

Day 7

I love Pizza Hut… the pizza balls are exceptional.

STRENGTH IS POWER

POSTED BY: SADDAM H.   AT 8:55 PM   (0) COMMENTS   PERMALINK ✉

comments

Day 8

Gained 12 pounds. I must stay strong. No food.

STRENGTH IS POWER

___

POSTED BY: SADDAM H.   AT 6:00 AM   (0) COMMENTS   PERMALINK ✉

comments

Day 9

Discovered vomiting.

STRENGTH IS POWER

POSTED BY: SADDAM H.   **AT 4:22 AM**   **(0) COMMENTS**   <u>**PERMALINK**</u>

comments

Day 10

I have an eating disorder. It's very serious. My American doctors say I binge eat, and then vomit. They suggest I end the hunger strike before I do irreversible damage to myself. They offered me a box of Kripsy Kremes to calm my stomach down. All the virgins in the world could not equal one bite of a glazed Krispy Kreme. Praise be Allah!

STRENGTH IS POWER

POSTED BY: SADDAM H.   **AT** 2:25 PM   (0) COMMENTS   <u>PERMALINK</u> ✉

comments

Day 11

I have ended the hunger strike. I believe it was successful in making the world aware of the injustice that I've endured during this trial. It's true that I have gained 17 pounds, but I was looking very gaunt on camera. Maybe the weight gain makes me seem more youthful and in charge ... like the old days. Other than my tongue turning a permanent day-glow reddish-orange (most likely from the chips) and developing type 2 diabetes, I feel reinvigorated.

STRENGTH IS POWER

POSTED BY: SADDAM H.   AT 7:44 AM   (0) COMMENTS   PERMALINK ✉

comments

GALLOWS HUMOR

SADDAMIZED FOR YOUR ENTERTAINMENT

What's the difference between Iraq and Vietnam?

Sand.

How do you keep an Iranian from drowning?

Apply electrodes to his genitals, beat him with a wire cable, cut his head off, chop off his arms and legs, feed his torso into a meat grinder, incinerate his clothing ... AND THEN throw him in the water!

Ten ways to know you might be a mongrel Kuwaiti dog:

You can lick your own balls

It is possible to scratch your ear with your foot

Leash

Flees

You eat from a bowl on the floor

Urge to raise leg to pee

Put nose in crotch to say "hello"

Recognize friends by ass smell

Barking

Eat your own poo (I've seen this many times with my own eyes)

What would you call Bush if 99% of his brain was missing?

Castrated

What do you get when you mix baked beans and falafel?

Tear gas

Why did the infidel soldier cross the road?

To find his arms and legs

How many suicide bombers does it take to screw in a light bulb?

No one knows, because suicide bombers don't last as long as a light bulb.

STRENGTH IS POWER

POSTED BY: SADDAM H.   AT 7:09 AM   (211) COMMENTS   PERMALINK ✉

comments

Damn Saddam those are some funny jokes you have told! My cousin and I are telling them all of the time sitting around the hookah down at the café. Here are some others you might enjoy to tell:

If Tarzan and Jane were Jewish what would Cheetah be?
– A fur coat.

What's the difference between Jesus and a painting?
– It only takes one nail to hang a painting.

What do you have when you've got six Iranians buried up to their necks in sand?
– Not enough sand.

Ha Ha keep up the good work and good luck in court.

Posted by: SheckyGreeneZone

Oh here's one more... A Kuwaiti goes into a psychiatrist's office and says, "Doc I have a problem. I think I'm a dog." The psychiatrist replies, "Oh my, that is bad. Please to lie on the couch so that I may do a diagnosis." Then the Kuwaiti says, "I can't I'm not allowed on the couch."

Posted by: SheckyGreeneZone

view more comments

A Kurd Judge Is A Pig Judge

Daily Trial Entry:

I hate this new judge, Rauf Abdul Rahman. He will not permit me to speak my mind on the fate of the crumbling Iraqi nation. It is because he is a Kurd. Kurds are not Iraqis, they are not even human, they are some sort of descendants of a pig. They are pigmen. Kurds live in Iraqi lands because I allow them to. They should be grateful that I tolerate their animal like ways. No country in the world would permit Kurds to live within their borders, but the Iraqi president's heart is big and generous, and I allow all these pigmen to live in my lands. And this Kurdish judge tells me what I can say and do. To hell with the pigman! I shall kill him and grind his flesh into headcheese or bacon, or some other pork by-product.

I wrote a song about him

> *My bologna has a first name*
> *It's R-A-O-U-F*
> *My bologna has a second name*
> *It's A-B-D-U-L-R-A-H-M-A-N*
> *I love to grind it every day*
> *And if you ask me why I'll saaaaayyyy*
> *'Cuz Raouf Abdul Rahman has a way with B-O-L-O-G-N-A*

STRENGTH IS POWER

POSTED BY: SADDAM H.   AT 6:55 PM   (0) COMMENTS   PERMALINK ✉

> comments

I Just Want To Be Loved By You

Daily Trial Entry:

I fear my strategies are weak. The public's opinion is sometimes against me...

. . . .

Americans want Saddam to hang if convicted
Most people in the United States want Saddam Hussein to hang if he's convicted at his trial, a view not shared by some longtime American allies... in the U.S., 57 percent, said Saddam should be executed...
– Associated Press

. . . .

Bloodthirsty American dogs, they want me executed. I don't deserve to die. I deserve to live! Thousands protested before Tookie Williams was put to death; why not me? Was it because he wrote a children's book? Well, I've written a children's book too. Here is an excerpt:

The Camel Herder and Quaboos
by Saddam Hussein

"Hi, Quaboos, you need to attend to the camels today," said the camel herder to Quaboos, his young apprentice.

"I would rather not," said Quaboos.

"I think you should," said the camel herder.

"No, I am busy with this stick. I am carving it into a mighty lion," said Quaboos.

"You can do that when all the camels have been fed," said the camel herder.

"But my stick has mighty powers," said the small boy.

"That's nice, Quaboos, but the camels need you now," said the camel herder.

"When I'm done with my stick, the camels will be fed instantly," said Quaboos.

"There is no time Quaboos. The camels are hungry and angry."

"Then I shall wave my magic stick now," said Quaboos.

Suddenly, all the Camels fell to the ground with a terrible thud. The camel herder became very angry and shouted, "The camels died Quaboos! You killed the camels!"

"I did not kill the camels, this stick killed the camels," said Quaboos.

"But you ordered the stick to kill the camels," said the angry camel herder.

"You are wrong. I simply waved the stick in the direction of the camels. I did not kill anything. I love camels. Why would I want to kill camels? They are my friends."

"Because you are a madman."

"No, I am not. I am a small boy with a magic stick who is being verbally abused by a big bully adult."

"Give me that stick."

"What stick?"

"That magic stick you just used to kill my camels."

"I have no stick. You make things up, old man."

"Where did you hide the stick?"

"I told you I have no stick."

"You made it disappear didn't you? You have some magic over it."

And the more the camel herder asked Quaboos where the stick was, the more Quaboos played with him. Sometimes he would bring out the stick, and sometimes he said he never had it. And no one knows to this day if Quaboos ever had a magic stick.

The End.

You see I have a children's story. I am in prison facing the death penalty. Now perhaps you will make a protest for me also.

STRENGTH IS POWER

POSTED BY: SADDAM H. **AT 10:12 PM** **(85) COMMENTS** **PERMALINK** ✉

comments

I am one of the unfortunate souls that read "Quaboos and the Camel Herder" to my boy. Recently, we walked through a sporting goods store and he grabbed a pair of ice skates. He held the blade against my throat and demanded I purchase them. He now owns a $350 pair of children's hockey skates.

But we live in Ramadi! In case you forgot, that's in the desert! I hope you hang. You bastard.

Posted by: SkatingOnSand

Hey, this Army General John Abizaid Commander of US Central Command. You have not responded to any of the emails or posts sent by our field officers regarding the orchestration of a covert escape and return to power.

Please advise ASAP. If you are inclined to the affirmative, at your next court appearance stand up, sit down, pull your hair, and wave your hands like you just don't care.

Posted by: GenJohn

view more comments

THE SADDAM DUMP

[Don't Believe The Hype]

I Am The Boogey Man

Daily Trial Entry:

Today, another pile of warrant-less accusations! The incrimination, insults, and blame, blame, blame. Everyone feels the need to place blame on me.

Then go ahead. I apparently can't stop you. Blame me. But it's not my fault. I am the victim! A proud man who happened to be trapped in many unhealthy relationships. Oh sure, in the beginning it seemed so wonderful. Reagan gave me helicopters. Clinton was so sweet. He called me all the time. Rumsfeld would drop by for a chat. Then everything fell apart, and I couldn't see how bad it was — people kept telling me, "you have to get out," but I just cared so much.

I really thought they could change. I tried everything. I held out rewards. I increased my oil output when they wanted it. I didn't cheat on them with the Soviets. Well, there was that one time, (how often do I have to apologize for that?) … they never gave me credit for anything.

Of course I tried threatening them too, but I only wanted them to pay attention to me again.

All these failed relationships, so heartbreaking. The lying, the deceit, the harsh words, and broken promises. They destroyed my self-esteem, and my self-worth. Now I know to call it for what it is: passive aggression *(W. – you reading this?)*. Do you blame me for being enabled *(Colin?)*, co-dependant? *(Donald – et tu Donald, et tu, et tu – nice dagger you got there Brutus, if only it wasn't sticking in my back!)*. And I don't use this word lightly … abusive. There I've said it. I am a victim of abuse. A.B.U.S.E. *(Dick – I still love you very, very much, but we should have stopped this a long time ago. I can't help you anymore)*.

Donny and me in better times, before we knew to call it co-dependence. Donald, why did you go so far out of your way to "help" me with my chemical problems? All the "covering" for me and "shading the truth," in the end it just made it worse, didn't it? So, so sad.

But you know what "*Mr. Giver of Justice*," "*Mr. Human Rights bla bla bla*," "*Mr. Everyone loves freedom crusader man*"? … if you need someone to blame that bad, if it's what you need to feel good about yourself, if your worldview is soooooo upset by how I chose to rule **MY COUNTRY**, then go ahead. Blame me. Saddam Hussein.

That's right, blame me for being a strong and just leader who understands and loves his people. Make me "A MONSTER". Go ahead, blame ME!

I am the boogey man. Boo!

– *Mind you, I'm not saying I'm guilty.*

SADDAM'S QUOTE CORNER

When I make speeches in my defense, I will need quotes to say I am honest and of good principles. These should be great words from the greatest men of our time, the words of my heroes, important words, words of power, and strength, and truth!

I will use their glorious meaning to inspire me and guide my arguments to victory. Here are a few to think about:

. . . .

...You need people like me so you can point your fucken' fingers and say, "That's the bad guy." So...what that make you? Good? You're not good. You just know how to hide, how to lie. Me, I don't have that problem. Me, I always tell the truth. Even when I lie. So say good night to the bad guy!
– *Al Pacino in SCARFACE*

Just had a great idea ... my life story done as a remake of *Scarface*!!! Should schedule time for screenplay after memoirs are done. Could be a great tie-in.

. . . .

The promise given was a necessity of the past: the word broken is a necessity of the present.
– *Niccolo Machiavelli*

See G.W. I get it.

. . . .

One death is a tragedy; a million is a statistic.
– *Joseph Stalin*

LOL – Gets funnier every time I read it.

You can't handle the truth... Son, we live in a world that has walls, and those walls have to be guarded by men with guns... And my existence, while grotesque and incomprehensible to you, saves lives. You don't want the truth because deep down in places you don't talk about at parties, you want me on that wall, you need me on that wall.
– Jack Nicholson in A FEW GOOD MEN

I too could have been a saver of lives, but unfortunately there aren't many walls in the desert? @%#$*!!

. . . .

What time is that train supposed to be here again?
– Benito Mussolini

Not sure why, but I just love this guy.

STRENGTH IS POWER

POSTED BY: SADDAM H.   AT 5:54 PM   (108) COMMENTS   PERMALINK ✉

comments

Saddam, I am a professor of psychology at Brandeis University, and I also have a family crisis therapy practice. I was moved by your heartfelt admission that you suffer from co-dependency issues. Being in abusive relationships can take time to overcome and I commend you for taking an important first step.

Treatment is a challenge but I assure you it does work. I suggest group therapy for all parties involved. If Mr. Rumsfeld, and the Bushes could sit down with you and maybe Chemical Ali could join us too, then we will be able to discuss your co-dependency in a warm and nurturing environment. It could be extremely beneficial.

For instance, you, Saddam, or even Chemical, might start by acknowledging that you brutally killed thousands of Iranian soldiers by dousing them with mustard gas. And then you, Donald, might admit that you covered for Saddam by rewarding him with a bonanza of American military hardware and full diplomatic relations soon after. The key for both of you is to learn to be self-reliant and just say "no."

Only then can true recovery take place and love and freedom take hold. I have next Thursday the 23rd open and would be willing to work with all of you.

Posted by: U_need_therapyUmmkay

Hey, what about me? HELLO... I was President when you invaded Iran...I never said a word. Do I get a little credit here? It's like I don't even exist. It figures.

Posted by: JimmyCarter

Hi Mr. Hussein, I'm a comedian and a sometime movie star. Well, it depends on your definition of movie star. My wife thinks I'm one, so maybe I am. You might have heard of me – Albert Brooks?

Anyway I was wondering if I could have just a few minutes of your time. I'm doing research on a new movie I'm writing, which I will also direct and act in. I'm calling it, "Finding Comedy in Abu Ghraib."

Thursday the 23rd looks good but I see you already have something booked. You think you might be free for lunch?

Posted by: NimosDad

I knew you were cheating on me all along.

Posted by: LeonidBreshnev

---

view more comments

My Spider Hole Vacation

Daily Trial Entry

The prosecutor today admonished me for running away, saying it was proof of my guilt. He said, "Who would spend months in a hole if they had nothing to hide? What were you going to do next? Lead a nationally televised slow speed chase driving a white Bronco with half the police force following you? Is that how you would show your innocence?"

He makes the O.J. joke on me? What a dolt! Well, the joke's on him. I have decided to write an essay and present it in court as evidence that I was on vacation.

What I Did On My Spider Hole Vacation.

By Saddam Hussein

The spider hole was excellent. I had my days to myself for once. No one came to me saying, "Oh Saddam, we have no money in the treasury after fighting one of the most expensive wars of the twentieth century." "Mr. President, the Kurds want to secede and keep all of their oil." "Excuse me Mr. Hussein, but we're going to need a kickback for letting you build that mosque instead of feeding your people and giving medicine to the children." Believe me, just not having to listen to that everyday was heaven.

Besides, I really enjoyed myself. No wifey. The kids were out of my hair. I did miss Uday and Qusay showing me additions to their severed body parts collection, but, other than that, I was happy to be living the bachelor's life again.

I could chill all day. I caught up on my reading. I joined Netflix and watched some great movies, and ordered in a lot of Domino's pizza.

After awhile I became bored though, so I decided to start hitting the local clubs in hopes of scoring some tribal tail. While I was excited to see if turning on the old Saddam razzle dazzle would still be enough to get me hooked up without the veiled threat of disembowelment, I figured venturing out would present one major problem.

Although I knew my people would never betray me, I would have to be wary of the infidels in our midst who might shoot me on sight. So I decided to leave the house only in disguise.

My disco disguises ... Early on I used a long beard, a little dirt, the bad boy bed-head and I was good to go. Soon, I noticed people staring, so I switched to the style of the "Godfather." Man, chicks went for it, but it took a long time to put together. Finally, I came up with a solution that worked best. I kept it simple and called myself "Nick."

All in all, it was a happy life for me on my spider hole vacation.

I had a little hut. I had a kitchen. One pot, one plate, a knife, a fork, a bottle and cork, very simple. I started to spend more and more time underground. It was good ... a great way to spend a day. I never felt more in touch with my own feelings and my own smell.

I have to admit I let things go a bit. Gained a few pounds and the days started to become hazy. Damn you Boone's Farm!

So when the Americans came for me, I have to admit it was a relief. It was time for this also to pass.

— *Must keep this ... it will make for a good entry in my memoirs.*

STRENGTH IS POWER

POSTED BY: SADDAM H.   **AT 4:52 PM**   **(211) COMMENTS**   **PERMALINK** ✉

i hate guys that bullshit and i hate cheap guys i need a man thats hard and knows what he wants.

luv to cam... i'm ready to show you right now baby... just $5 for 24hrs i do what ever you want to seee... pic on my profile at myspace mssg me with ""1234 so i know ur serious all others will be ignored to get ahold of me yahoo handle: AnytimeAnita512

Posted by: KinkyGrrrl

To KinkyGrrrl: You sound really fantastic. I tried your handle and didn't get a msg. Back??? Do you do costume? I'm looking for an Ann Coulter role-play – you: Nazi SS shewolf, long blonde wig. Me: blue leather chaps, spank me, call me a liberal and force me to watch FOX.

Do you take Amex?

Posted by: RangerRed

view more comments

Limericks By Saddam

Interlude:

There once was a man from Tikrit
Who the armies of Satan couldn't defeat
He rode into power on his uncle's back
Dropped dissenters like a UFC champion on crack
Then put the leftovers in grinders of meat

I like hookers
And curious on-lookers
My life is a show
Filled with cash and mountains of blow
I like hookers

I had a son named Uday
I also had a son named Qusay
They were wicked and bad
And one day they asked, dad…
Can we go out and kill some people and rape some virgins and rob some
banks and do a pile of drugs and mess up the local economies of a few
small towns and blame it on people we don't know hoping that you will
then kill them to cover up what we did?

– Damn I loved those kids.

Iraq is a country I love
But the Americans dropped bombs from above
So I had to hide in a dirt filled hole
Until I landed in court playing this role
I wish I had Johnny Cochran and a small bloody glove

STRENGTH IS POWER

POSTED BY: SADDAM H.   AT 12:36 AM   (0) COMMENTS   PERMALINK ✉

comments

You Must Have Good Pre-nup

Note To Self:

Get a good prenuptial agreement. Always!

. . . .

Samira Shahbandar, "...is believed to have given the Americans and their allies some information about the area where Saddam was hiding," the sources said.
– *Mail & Guardian*

. . . .

So it was my ex-wife Samira, the whore daughter of a camel dung shoveller, who turned me in — I am shocked! I thought I had an ironclad pre-nup. This proves that you must have a good lawyer. Stay away from those Internet lawyers ... I thought I filled in all the fields properly, but I must have missed one.

It was all there: if we should part ways, she gets to keep the Hummer Limousine, the Basra palace, $272 million (I know ... a paltry sum, but she was not there with me during my early years when I acquired the bulk of my wealth). Also, she can't testify against me in any trial, she can't give interviews to *People Magazine* or the *National Enquirer* about our life together, but, somehow I forgot to put in "if she happens to be captured by the world's only super power, she can not reveal my hideout." How could I have been so stupid? And I thought I had included everything.

STRENGTH IS POWER

POSTED BY: SADDAM H.   AT 12:36 AM   (14) COMMENTS   PERMALINK ✉

Comments:

Screw you! I can't believe you paraded me around like that. Your secrets are not safe with me, you bastard! And I was there when you earned a lot more money than that. You took the Kirkuk oil fields and diverted almost half the money to Swiss Bank accounts while I was your wife. That's billions you bastard. It was my idea! And you only can give me a measly $272 million. What kind of man are you? I am the mother of your only living son, how are we supposed to live? Huh?

And look at you now, in a cell, where you belong! There were 70 palaces, and Ali and I only get one! You cheap son of goat herder! And where is my jewelry? You took my jewelry! I want back the Cartier diamond-studded bracelet that you probably gave to that whore, the one you had traipsing around in my palaces – yeah, the palaces that I designed, not you.

Do you think you would have the taste to gold plate the showerheads? You can never know such taste. You're too busy having your portrait painted, or putting new medals on your military uniforms, or having your moustache waxed – although I must admit it is very sexy. Oh how you would twirl it for me when you were in uniform, with the beret...

I must have you back! I can't take it. For the love of Allah just one more night of ecstasy! Please!!!!

POSTED BY: SamiraBaby

view more comments

Saddam Is Most Popular

Daily Trial Entry

I must listen another day to lies about how I torture and kill my people … these are lies! I am a loving man. I love the people of Iraq. How do you stay in power 35 years unless your people love you? My people love me! I am their president.

These American dogs do not know unadulterated love for their leader. Bush, with his 34% approval rating, can't have any idea what it is to be loved by the people. Not even during the retreat from Kuwait did I receive a 34% approval rating. My rating was always in the high 90's. The polls that were taken are proof. Here is just one:

In march 1992, one thousand Iraqis were taken into the Ministry of Information and asked the following questions.

Participants were asked to respond YES, NO, or UNSURE	0	500	1000	
Do you agree with Saddam Husseins' policy to keep UN Weapons Inspectors out of his palaces?	Y			899
	N			4
	U			97
Is Saddam Hussein doing a great job governing Iraq?	Y			896
	N			3
	U			0
Do you believe that Saddam Hussein is the reincarnated King of Babylonia?	Y			634
	N			3
	U			256
Are you convinced that Iraq is the rightful heir to the southwest corridor of Iran and all of Kuwait?	Y			370
	N			1
	U			4
Do you think Saddam Hussein should serve another 35 years?	Y			365
	N			0
	U			0

After polling was complete all participants were returned to their families.

Now that is love!

STRENGTH IS POWER

POSTED BY: SADDAM H.   AT 11:44 AM   (0) COMMENTS   PERMALINK ✉

comments

Raising Kids

Advice:

I have received numerous emails praising me for the job I did raising my sons. Child rearing is the hardest part of being a president; there is so little time to be with your family when you are caring for a great nation. I needed to learn quick and effective parenting skills for my sons to obey me. I'm glad to share these skills with the fans of this blog.

> I am having trouble raising my children. They won't listen to me. They are not loyal to the family and do not take advice. You seemed to have done such a good job with Uday and Qusay. They did everything for you. They even killed for you. I can't get my son to clean up the dog sh*t in the back yard and it's his dog!
>
> Any tips?
>
> Umar

My Arab brother, I feel your pain. You should never tolerate such insolence. Next time that happens, you grab your son's head and bring him to the doody. You need to shove his face in it as you repeatedly smack him with a newspaper. I promise he will never do it again. If he doesn't clean it up again, you put his arm in a wood chipper.

Also, hanging your children upside down for extended periods teaches them important lessons. You can decide what lessons.

> I am so mad at my 14 year-old son. He rode his bike today and forgot to put on his kneepads and shoulder pads, although he did have his helmet on. The other day he went a whole block down the street to a friend's house without adult supervision. They are so fragile. I can't even watch when he flies kites for fear of electrocution or strangulation.
>
> What am I supposed to do? How do I get him to be more careful?
>
> Tammy from America

Tammy, you need to let him grow up. Do you really want your kid becoming a Big American Wimp. I suggest you send your son on an illegal small arms trade to Africa. This is a rite of passage in the Hussein family. I know of no other way to make them men. Although I lost one son in Liberia, most have come back stronger and ready to conquer the world.

> My kid continues to do poorly in school and just sits around all the time watching the Cartoon Network. I fear he won't be able to earn a living as an adult.
> Please help!
> Taahir

Don't worry Taahir. There are ways. I remember I couldn't get Ali (Son of my second wife) to stop playing his video games. I felt he was missing out on real life, you know, kid's stuff: walks around the palace, being chauffeured around Baghdad in a limo, going with his mother to Paris on a shopping spree. But instead he just sat in his room playing those stupid video games.

It was especially upsetting because he was playing a video game called "Desert Storm." All day and night I had to hear Iraqi soldiers being killed like cockroaches, followed by his constant cheering. I was so mad. Finally I told him, if you don't go outside and play with your security guards, I'm going to destroy that machine.

It is unfortunate that I had to exile him for 3 months to a famine stricken village in the Republic of Congo, but when he came back, he never played video games again. I could see him on the palace grounds kicking the ball to my Chief of Police and then blowing up toads with firecrackers along the Tigris — just a regular boy.

STRENGTH IS POWER

POSTED BY: SADDAM H.   AT 8:42 AM   (0) COMMENTS   PERMALINK ✉

comments

A New Career Path?

Note To Self:

It is possible that when I am found innocent I might not get my country back. So I am considering other career options. I think I'd make an excellent international consultant.

It's amazing that no one ever asks me anything. I've been in the middle of the Middle East for 35 years, and I might know a few things. So any prospective employer, take note: Here's the pipeline I prepared of the latest international strategies that provide real added value to any multinational corporate entity in need of serious R&D.

Pakistan: Mushareff, I can't stand the guy. He thinks he is smart, but is a real idiot, more stupid than George Bush. He calls himself a general, but name any war that he's fought in ... I've killed more people on a Tuesday

Syria: Nice country. Assad is a very good pool player, I enjoy his tricycle collection

The Russians: Drink a lot, poor health, weapons stink (although AK 47's are pretty cool), get long terms, never pay in full. The Americans will eventually start a war, which will void all the contracts.

The Germans: They'll sell you anything ... except Audis.

Saudi Arabia: King Faud, he farts a lot. Can't stand to be in the same room with him after a bowl of hummus.

French: Very accommodating, easy to do oil deals with (especially when UN's involved). Be careful with their nukes. Customer service is rude and will only speak French. Nice whores.

China: Disturbingly little.

United States: A lot of saber rattling. Wusses. Never follow through. Will always cut and run. Haven't won a real war in 60 years.

The best strategy: goad them into battle, sustain heavy casualties and tremendous loss of infrastructure, hold on for 5 or 6 years, and they'll rebuild your country better than it was.

STRENGTH IS POWER

POSTED BY: SADDAM H.   AT 12:59 PM   (0) COMMENTS   PERMALINK ✉

comments

THE SADDAM DUMP

[Here Comes The Rain]

Ramsey's "So What" Defense

Daily Trial Entry:

This was in the *LA Times* op-ed the other day about one of my *legal* advisors…

. . . .

Ramsey Clark: Saddam Hussein's Chief Apologist

In an interview with the BBC last week and another in the *New York Times* on Tuesday, Clark addressed the charge that in 1982, after an apparent attempt on his life in the Iraqi town of Dujail, Saddam had ordered the torture and murder of about 150 men and boys from the area.

Far from denying that any such horror had occurred, Clark asserted that it was justifiable. He has now twice said in public that, given the war with the Shiite republic of Iran, Saddam was entitled to take stern measures. "He had this huge war going on, and you have to act firmly when you have an assassination attempt," he told the BBC…

Christopher Hitchens, LA Times

. . . .

Brilliant! *So what!* Of course I did it; who can blame me?

This is a defense? I murdered everyone … so what? — The "so what defense!" Is this the best the former Attorney General of the United Sates of America can come up with?

Ramsey suiting up for court

So What? SO WHAT?!!!! Are you kidding me?

I should kill him myself before the eyes of the court and international press. And as I strangle the last breath out of his flopping, worthless corpse, I will smile and say, "Saddam was entitled to take stern measures. He had this huge trial going on, and you have to act firmly when you have an incompetent lawyer."

Actually this might work. Everyone hates lawyers.

STRENGTH IS POWER

POSTED BY: SADDAM H.   AT 6:49 PM   (101) COMMENTS   PERMALINK ✉

comments

Dude! I'm totally with ya on your court strategy! I did the same thing for my DUI trial. (I'll be out in only 9 more months)

Drunk Drivers Against Mad Mothers!!!!!!

Posted by: D-DAMM

view more comments

I Require A Puppet Lawyer

Daily Trial Entry:

I have decided to take charge and advertise for new attorneys. Here is my posting on Monster.com:

Attorney Wanted: A world-class leader of an authoritarian regime is currently forming a team of trial lawyers to appear in a puppet court created by the world's only superpower.

Requirements: At least five years experience defending a despot, tyrant, autocrat, dictator or tribal leader charged with crimes against humanity, ethnic cleansing, torture, and/or various book-keeping irregularities.

Should speak some Arabic, be familiar with the new Iraqi law, and be willing to be encased in a Kevlar body suit on a daily basis for up to 15 years.

Compensation: The successful candidate will receive as compensation for a "not guilty" verdict: three palaces, a case of rubies, and five percent of the world's second largest oil reserves.

In the event of a guilty verdict: you will get to keep the Kevlar body suit.

Only Ivy League need apply.

No Jews.

As you can see in this photo, my new lawyers will have to have experience working in a puppet court.

STRENGTH IS POWER

POSTED BY: SADDAM H.   **AT 12:29 AM**   (79) **COMMENTS**   <u>PERMALINK</u> ✉

At Menckle, Menckle, and Myerwitz we have never handled a crimes against humanity case before. But we do specialize in defending rapists. It's all pretty much the same thing anyway. We obtain innocent verdicts the old fashioned way: we break down your victims on the stand and expose their sultry past.

We've gotten off more than 300 rapists, and 38 sexual predators – wait that doesn't sound right. Anyway, if you add up these numbers it comes pretty damn close to equaling one "crimes against humanity" charge. Think about it.

BTW you'll have to make an exception on the Jewish thing. Maybe we can do a discount rate if it makes you feel better.

Posted by: MartyLaw

This is CENTCOM Commander Army Gen. Abizaid again. You are one tough negotiator. We are offering you an opportunity here to put you back in power. Why won't you respond?!!!! What the hell do you want? We are willing to let you go! Set you back up again! You want your palaces cleaned up – you got it! You want your weapons back, no problem! We'll even toss in some WMDs no questions asked.

BTW your new signal is: pat your head, rub your stomach, and honk your nose.

Posted by: GenJohn

---

view more comments

Jury of My Peers

Daily Trial Entry:

I demand a jury of my peers! I am the leader of an Arab nation so it is only fair that I be judged by other great Arab leaders. All I ask is the same justice that a person can find in any American courtroom. These are my peers, and they are the only ones qualified to decide my innocence.

Egyptian President Hosni Mubarak: 25 years of uninterrupted service as President of Egypt, is unbiased in his leanings, should make an excellent juror.

Libyan Revolutionary Leader Colonel Muammar Qadhafi: He is in the business of oil and weapons development – a genuine peer. He has the experience: as leader of Libya for 37 years he really understands the pitfalls of leading an Arab nation and surviving a direct hit from the American war machine… making him the most qualified peer of the bunch.

Syrian President Bashar al-Asad: Leads a nation that shares a common border with Iraq, knows the problems of keeping law & order while providing safe residence for terrorist groups and trading in illegal arms – a wonderful international spokesperson for peace… could truly be impartial.

Palestinian Prime Minister Ismail Haniyeh: A great Hammas leader, completely dedicated to the destruction of Israel. He came up the hard way through murder and intimidation… if ever there was one to judge me it is this man.

Former Secretary of State Colin Powell: My attorneys remind me that we will have to approve a few jurors from the prosecution's list. In preparation I have selected Mr. Powell. After his performance in front of the UN Security Council, we can expect him to draw fantastic conclusions from circumstantial evidence when given the right incentive… we'll probably have to accept at least one token anyway.

STRENGTH IS POWER

POSTED BY: SADDAM H.   AT 2:54 PM   (201) COMMENTS   PERMALINK ✉

In regards to your selection of Colin Powell, please do not add the modifier African to precede American when classifying the nature of your so-called "token." We kicked him out of that club years ago.

Posted by: L_Farrakhan

Why limit yourself to your close neighbors, Saddam? As the leader of Sudan, I'm just a stone's throw away and I've been named number one for two years running in Parade Magazine's top ten world's worst dictators. Between the Janjaweed militia and my military we've burned so many villages and killed so many people in Dafur that there isn't anything left to kill or burn.

The good news is we're working on the refugee camps now. So shouldn't I be considered too? I think it would be nice to do my civic duty and sit on the jury of your peers.

Posted by: Omar_al-Bashir

Saddam, you should pick me for this jury sometime. I have "reeducation camps," my people suffer malnourishment, and I kill anyone who look at me funny.

Did I mention I have disco shoe too. We party long time.

Posted by: DearLeader

I agree with Omar_al-Bashir, why limit yourself? Name: Than Shwe, Burma. Credentials: largest conscription army in the world, most are under age 12. I don't really go in for rape rooms and torture, but I do use forced labor on almost all public works.

Posted by: BigBoy-n-Burma

I worship you! In fact, I recently purchased on eBay the middle finger from a bronze statue of you that stood in Basra. It is my most prized possession.

Posted by: I_Heart_Saddam

---

view more comments

I Pardon Myself

Daily Trial Entry:

As the freely elected President of the Republic of Iraq, and with the full authority granted to me by the Constitution of said Republic, I hereby pardon myself of all crimes against the Iraqi people, including but not limited to:

Thievery, torture, rape, pillaging, dismemberment, gassing, stealing, being mean, land grabbing, ethnic cleansing, mass murder, cherry bellies, political assassinations, hanging, carving, gouging, poking, mocking, derision, public humiliation, battery, psychological torture, brain freezes, purple nurples, wife killings, false imprisonment, emotional torture, sexual beatings, ritual rape, toenail removal, rectum stretching, spreading cooties, shooting weapons in large crowds, polygamy, bad taste, and hoarding.

STRENGTH IS POWER

POSTED BY: SADDAM H. AT 6:01 AM   (0) COMMENTS   PERMALINK ✉

comments

I Drop The Mic

Dogmatic Rambling:

I feel more empowered and in touch with the Iraqi people than at any other time of my presidency. And I owe it all to this blog. Blogging is the best way for a president to communicate his true desires since the advent of public executions.

It so beats standing in front of all those formal Baath Party Congresses and "addressing the people" – so last millennium. I would say one line, and then I would have to stand there for 20 minutes while I got a standing ovation. And then I would be compelled to carefully watch the hall to see who would sit down first. You start to lose your focus. It stops becoming about the speech but whom you must murder in the next few minutes. It's a terrible way to communicate.

A simple blog entry, and I can communicate with thousands on a much more intimate level. It is a superior form of communication – much better than showing up at some rally at a Baghdad Square with thousands of adoring Iraqis screaming "Saddam! Saddam!" About the only thing you can get out is an occasional "Death to America!" and, if you're lucky, maybe "America is the Great Satan." Nothing more. And this is after hours of getting ready. Attaching all those pesky medals to your military uniform takes a half hour alone. Then there's all the clean up – they never show you that. You should see what that place looks like the next day. Empty shotgun shells everywhere, half-burned American flags, vultures feeding on trampled corpses, remnants of scorched giant paper-maché heads of George W. – the place is a disaster.

STRENGTH IS POWER

POSTED BY: SADDAM H.   AT 3:00 PM   (0) COMMENTS   PERMALINK ⊠

comments

Winning In The Court Of Public Opinion

Daily Trial Entry:

I have been thinking my ways are old fashioned. I cannot hope to sway this tribunal to believe in my innocence by making flowery speeches, invoking the Koran, or delivering pronouncements of their irrelevance. No, I need a new approach. I will think differently on the outside of a box.

I will win this thing in the court of public opinion.

This is why I have hired a publicist. She says she will be my own personal "Blossoming Turd." This is revolting. But I do want to learn the ways of the modern news spinner, so I let it pass and focused on her media plan.

Objective: Intimidate potential witnesses, influence the decisions of the court, polarize the population and foment civil unrest, affect world politics, in three words: save my ass.

Stay on message: I am innocent. Doesn't matter what I did. I didn't do it.

Speak to talking points: The judges are monkeys. The witnesses are lying. I am the victim. And there are people out there a lot worse than me.

Use one Media outlet: All communications should go to one and only one news outlet. This is simple – Al Jazeera loves me.

I am the number one daytime show in the Middle East. Here it is an obsession.

While watching me at a café, this man shows his exuberance by firing his pistol. I am flattered but it did not work out well for the mother of three living upstairs.

Use "straw man" tactics: This at first was confusing to me. But as my publicist explained the straw man is made for you to knock down. Really, it is a simple thing. Start your sentences with, "some people say…" then make an assertion based on your opponent's beliefs but exaggerate them to the verge of comedy. And then make the point you wish to drive home. No matter how ridiculous your views are they sound great when compared to the "straw man."

– I wonder if there are tin man, or lion tactics. I wish to be a lion.

Politics of fear: Check.

Discredit the opposition: I think it is well known that the judges are transvestite lovers.

Leak, leak, leak: This reminds me of a good joke. What do old people smell like? – Depends.

I feel better already. Because the publicist has helped me put everything in perspective, this will be a walk on cake.

STRENGTH IS POWER

POSTED BY: SADDAM H.   AT 11:33 AM   (0) COMMENTS   PERMALINK ✉

comments

116

THE SADDAM DUMP

[Brass Tacks And Bare Knuckles In Baghdad]

My Falling Down House

Daily Trial Entry:

Because of the recent escalation of violence, my lawyers have made a motion to grant postponement at once. Civil war is upon us and I am needed more than ever to save the union. The Americans must free me now! It is time for me to take my rightful place in history and keep Iraq from splitting in two or even three, or quite possibly 17.

The Americans know too well that only a great leader can save a nation faced with a civil war. I am that great man. I am the freely elected president of Iraq. Most of my children died while I was in office and my wife went insane or is missing. I have a beard.

Could it be any clearer? — I am a man of destiny.

Ramsey does not believe the motion will do much good but the court must let me go so that I may lead my people through this Civil War!

Just in case the court is made sensible, I have written a speech:

> *Three score and 5 years ago, our founding father, me, brought forth upon this Middle East, a new nation, conceived in limited freedom, and dedicated to the proposition that "some men are created equal." Now that we are engaged in a great civil war, testing whether a*

group of fanatic crazed Muslims can endure longer than a group of insane radical Islamists.

We are met on a great battlefield of that war, Ajabi's Vegetable Stand at 86th & 4th. We have come to dedicate a portion of that market, as a shallow grave for those who gave their lives that this nation might live. The brave men, living and dead, who struggled here, have hallowed it, far above our poor power to add or detract. The world will little note, nor long remember, what we say here, while it can never forget what they did here.

– They blew themselves up!

We resolve that this nation, under Allah, shall have a new birth of subjugation, and that government of the zealots, by the extremists, for the insurgents, run by me shall not perish from the earth.

STRENGTH IS POWER

POSTED BY: SADDAM H. AT 9:45 PM (69) COMMENTS PERMALINK ⊠

comments

You are greater than Lincoln. He only appears on the $5 bill and the lowly penny. You appear on every piece of Iraqi currency. Please, he could only wish to appear on the 1000 Dinar.

Posted by: AliFrom7-11

As the proprietor of Yusuf & Sons, Baghdad's Finest Mortuary, I want to thank you for the great customers you've sent my way over the years. The idea of going all-out with civil war is pure marketing genius. It'll put our sales through the roof. And I thought business was good when you were in power – this is unbelievable.

Posted by: UKill-emWeBox-em

view more comments

A President In Need Is A President Indeed

Advice:

I was looking through the many warm emails and posts this morning (thank you so much everyone) and I came across this email. It just breaks your heart, don't it?

> Hello Saddam,
>
> I am President Ilham Aliyev, of the Republic of Azerbaijan. I have only served a few years as the freely elected ;-) president of my country, and quite honestly I am struggling to maintain an iron grip on the nation.
>
> There are just so many groups that want to take me out that it is simply overwhelming. Everyone from the opposition parties to International Human Rights Organizations, to that gap-toothed American jezebel Condoleezza Rice.
>
> Your thoughts?

Ilham – I can help

I appreciate your situation. It is very difficult for one man to control the many without first understanding a few simple rules. Therefore, I have compiled a list of pointers for you and any other fledgling "freely elected" president that wishes to rule his people with the same command that I have shown for over 3 decades:

The 10 Pillars of Leading a Nation

1.) Proclaim free elections but keep it to just one candidate.

2.) ALWAYS SPEAK LOUDLY, NO MATTER HOW CLOSE PEOPLE ARE STANDING.
– Remember you can get what you want by simply yelling vicious threats.

3.) Grow a moustache.

4.) Declare "I have weapons of mass destruction."

5.) Do business with the United Nations.
– UN mixers are a great place to network with other "freely elected" presidents.

6.) Maintain a proper number of body doubles but remember who they are.

7.) Put your face on everything, including the labels of fish food.

8.) Announce "I have no weapons of mass destruction."

9.) Embrace the religion of your people.
– But not to the point where you actually have to participate in it.

10.) Have sons you can control, the stupider, the better.

11.) Grant interviews to Dan Rather only.

12.) Proclaim "I definitely have weapons of mass destruction."

13.) Wear a military uniform on all occasions.

14.) Blame the Zionists and Americans for everything.

15.) Befriend Hollywood celebrities.
– Preferably A-list, no Kato Kaelins. That could do damage.

16.) Be seen holding babies.

17.) Only use torture when it is absolutely necessary, for instance, when a group of people tries to kill you, which will be often.

18.) Mark your torture victims.
– You don't want to waste time and have to torture them again … believe me, once is enough.

19.) If you need more pillars, add them. They're cheap.

STRENGTH IS POWER

POSTED BY: SADDAM H.   AT 2:15 PM   (115) COMMENTS   PERMALINK ✉

I was a member of the Republican Guard and I have not received any benefit pay in 3 years. The steel plate in my head has rusted and desperately needs replacing. And no one takes the Republican Guard Vet Card anymore.

I have written to the head of the Republican Guard Veterans Administration, but he was executed last spring. We are a forgotten bunch. There are no parades for us. We were the 4th largest army in the world, the "mother of all armies." I am an Iranian War Vet, Kuwaiti War Vet and "whatever they're calling this war" Vet. Please help me with any spare change you may have.

Posted by: SleepingUnderaBush-n-Baghdad

Hey it's Kato, why are you ragging on me? You can't believe the tail I get. Things are on the move; things are in the groove. I just did a KCAL Ch. 9 News segment, I got a shot on "I Love the 90's," and I co-host a new reality courtroom series, "Eye for an Eye." By the way you look great? I like the beard.

In fact, I'm the only celebrity that can actually help you. Our Judge, Extreme Akim, settles cases in under 7 minutes. I could probably get you on the show – now that's some real Hollywood clout for you. However, there's a small catch: if you lose, you have to spend a day in the other person's shoes. Pretty wild concept, huh?

So, if you are willing to be gassed to death 7000 times before the 2nd commercial break we would love to have you on. No pressure just a thought. Give me a buzz, if you ever need a roommate.

Posted by: Kaelin36

Do you think I could come out of the Torture Box now? It's been 12 years and you're not even in charge anymore.

Posted by: BonsaiKamil

---

view more comments

123

How Shallow

Daily Trial Entry:

They claim that I have murdered many Iraqis and buried them in shallow graves. But the Americans keep finding new shallow graves, and I no longer get blamed. Are mine not shallow enough? Do they not go deep enough? How do they know whose shallow graves are whose? You can't have it both ways. I can't be accused of mass murder, and then, when another shallow grave is found, have somebody else get the credit.

Do the Americans just assign shallow graves to whomever they need to blame that week? This is crazy. Is this the chart that the American military uses to determine who's responsible for which deaths?

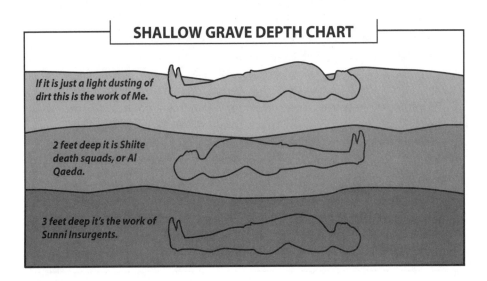

SHALLOW GRAVE DEPTH CHART

If it is just a light dusting of dirt this is the work of Me.

2 feet deep it is Shiite death squads, or Al Qaeda.

3 feet deep it's the work of Sunni Insurgents.

When "eliminating" a problem, remember to always bury the bodies. How deep is up to you.

STRENGTH IS POWER

POSTED BY: SADDAM H.   **AT** 7:31 AM   **(0) COMMENTS**   PERMALINK ✉

comments

124

Do The Generalissimo

Advice:

A man should dress for success. He should not walk into a department store and look at prices. He should know what he's doing, and what he wants to accomplish. A nice gabardine or worsted wool can make you feel and look like a billion dollars.

But nothing compares to the military uniform, preferably in a one hundred percent cotton khaki, to give a man a sense of power and control.

I like this outfit when I'm trying to crack down on dissenters, or lounging around the pool area with my female friends. It is especially effective with your people when you are still wearing it and your country is no longer at war. A wide selection of cleanly pressed military uniforms with appropriate medals can assure a very successful night with the ladies.

Accessories:

Very Large Reading Glasses

Sometimes I will wear large reading glasses with the military uniform. They will give your look a grandfatherly feel, this is very effective. It takes the edge off the implied threat of military action, while providing a softer touchiness.

A Fur Hat, And Long Black Overcoat

Admittedly this is borrowed from Stalin's repertoire, but it is classic and stylish. I highly recommend it when you must send a message to the world that you are one crazy motherfucker.

Armani Suit

My Armani suit is a great change of pace. It gives me a sense of style, and commands respect from my Western friends. This is a great outfit when you want to give an air of civility. It's especially effective when you're purchasing dual-use equipment from European leaders, and you want to assure them that you have no plans to use the neutron generators as components in a crude gun-implosion nuclear device.

STRENGTH IS POWER

POSTED BY: SADDAM H.   AT 4:23 AM   (0) COMMENTS   PERMALINK ✉

comments

Pimp Your Palace

Advice:

This entry is not so much about the trial. It becomes tedious and bores me. In the days before my incarceration, when the country was run properly, the justice system was swift. The process of arrest / torture / questioning / torture / trial / conviction / torture / execution / dismemberment / shallow grave could be handled many times in a single day.

Praise be to Allah for this web log. It sustains me and keeps my mind alert. As the site grows and I get to know more of my online supplicants, one man has caught my attention and imagination. His name is Thomas Wheelwright of Beaumont Texas. His is a harrowing story of survival, perseverance, and a love of overstuffed velveteen love seats, gold filigreed rococo accents, and leopard skin throw pillows – a man truly after my own heart.

His first email reads in part:

> "...big fan of the site, nice work. I was wondering seeing how you used to have a new palace built like every other week, how is it you had time to design, build, and especially do the interior decorating? And you did all of this while invading other countries, putting down internal resistance, and manipulating world energy policy.
>
> Wow! You must have great multi-tasking skills.
>
> I watch a lot of Extreme Home Makeover with Ty Pennington. It is one of my favorite shows, and I love what they do, but they don't have your sense of grandeur and style. Since you have more time on your hands now I was hoping you might share some of your design and construction experience..."

Thomas is a humble man. After sharing the correspondence with him, the total of his need became clear to me.

While working as a process engineer in the munitions numbering department of a Texas Instruments' subsidiary, Thomas was faced with a life and death emergency. A robotic arm malfunctioned on the assembly floor, threatening to cover two hundred female line workers of "Mexican descent" with a toxic mix of Tributyltin, Polyvinyl Chloride, and Aluminum Oxides. With only seconds to decide between his own safety and the relative expense of replacing valuable company "resources," Thomas knew what he had to do.

He plunged his hand into the lower swing pivot, hoping to disable the control servo unit. The machine devoured his entire right arm and the three primary digits of his left hand. Locking-up on torn flesh and broken bone it did not come to a complete stop before discharging the entire reservoir of chemical curing agents onto Thomas' head.

During Thomas' three months of hospitalization, occupational therapy, and decontamination, tragedy struck again. His sister died of sudden heart failure, leaving him with her three adopted children. His own twin daughters were diagnosed with a rare form of leukemia. And then news came that, because Thomas was "work for hire," the insurance company would only cover the first one hundred dollars of his medical expenses.

The Wheelwright family has been through a lot, but the biggest problem came when they lost everything that was near and dear to them when their house literally exploded. Sherry, Thomas' wife, was in the house at the time. She is dead.

I am so proud of Thomas. With only the thumb and pinky finger of his left hand to work with, and the generous support of a few Islamic charities I know, he was able to rebuild his life and create the dream house only I could imagine.

After his release from the hospital and collecting the various children in his charge, Thomas moved into this cramped two-room single-wide.

I told him, "What ever your lot in life ... build on it!"

The first thing Thomas needed to conquer was the problem of a larger plot on which to build his "palace." Ordinarily I would have suggested a dispute based on ethnic or religious differences that would lead to annexation. But as luck would have it, a tornado did the work for him. At least everything in life does not have to be tragedy for the Wheelwrights.

With land still at a premium, I toned down the size of the Wheelwright palace and designed upwards. A towering palace can send a message to the community that you are the big dog in the yard.

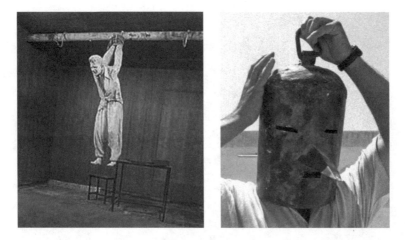

Unquestionably, the most daunting challenge facing Thomas was suddenly becoming a single parent of three little girls and two rambunctious boys. The new floor plan was designed as a labyrinth of corridors, spiral staircases, trap doors, and secret compartments. While this is perfect for boys, it is a logistical disaster, making surveillance of young girls impossible. With the addition of a special "playroom" where they could be placed for weeks or months at a time, the problem was solved. The picture above shows workmen testing the playroom and some of its toys just prior to the Wheelwright's move-in.

When Thomas first moved into the trailer, his biggest complaint was that the kitchen / bathroom / living room was so small and dysfunctional that there were times that he couldn't hear the thoughts in his own head for the screaming of the children. In three words... Thomas needed space! As a result, Thomas was thrilled with the addition of the contemplation room. It is a perfect place to ruminate about world domination, and the beauty of intercontinental ballistic missiles.

By paying attention to details like a Wedgwood china bidet, fantasy paintings on velvet, and an old-school gold chariot, I made Thomas' dream palace a reality.

– It's nice to be a giver.

STRENGTH IS POWER

My Conventional Is Not Your Conventional

Daily Trial Entry:

I saw this in the news today and felt I must respond...

. . . .

We know Saddam used WMDs on his own people
– Taegon Goddards Political Wire

The Baath regime threatened, responded by destroying Kurdish villages... These brutal conventional measures failed to achieve their objective, and for that reason the Baath regime initiated its chemical warfare on the Kurds in 1988.
– History News Network

. . . .

I only used conventional weapons, if ever. Your American dictionary defines "conventional" as meaning "conforming or adhering to accepted standards as of conduct or taste." As president of Iraq, a country of 27 million people located in the Middle East, I only used weapons that conformed to the accepted standards and tastes of the Arab World.

Our "conventional" may not be your "conventional." In our "conventional," captives heads are routinely cut off and suicide bombers blow themselves up with rat poison-soaked nails to induce a slow and horrifying death. These are the conventional weapons used in our region.

I only used conventional weapons!

STRENGTH IS POWER

POSTED BY: SADDAM H.   **AT 6:16 PM**   **(41) COMMENTS**   **PERMALINK** ✉

comments

We're very interested in these "conventional weapons" you speak of but we don't have a lot of space. Let me ask you, if the wind suddenly shifts, can the gas blow back on you. That would be very bad.

Posted by: Prez_o_Hammas

Well if this is true that would mean that my Uncle's AK 47 is not really that bad. Maybe like my Dad's shotgun or something, and that would mean that my Dad's Shotgun is more like my older brother's 22 rifle, which would mean that his 22 rifle would be like a water pistol. Wow I can't wait to go shoot at my cousins in the backyard this weekend – awesome!

Posted by: SkooterShoter

Hey, I don't know how much longer I can hold onto to these things... some of the radioactive stuff is leaking.... And the mustard gas stinks!

Posted by: SnuckIt2Syria

---

view more comments

THE SADDAM DUMP

[The End Is Near]

Plea Bargaining

Daily Trial Entry:

It might be time to bargain a plea. It is a tradition of Middle-East culture to barter. I have things they wish to know, and they have things I wish to have. So here's my deal: I will admit to gassing the Kurds (didn't do it), the illegal invasion of Kuwait (they had it coming), and the one hundred fifty executions in Dujail (I make the laws in this country, and trying to kill me is definitely against the law).

Plus, I will throw in the location of three hundred sixty-two shallow grave sites including: three large pits of missing arms, the location of the entire University of Baghdad's 1982 political studies class, and the '78 Olympic Soccer Team, a warehouse of heads, a two mile trench filled with bad restaurateurs, a cave of toes, and a cement-filled tunnel of my ex-wives, oh, and a farm house containing twenty-eight carets of uncut diamonds.

In return, I ask that I be exiled to French Guiana with full citizenship and protection. I would also expect to receive what any other formerly disgraced world leader is given: I get to occasionally appear as a commentator on CNN and Fox News. I get to make speeches around the world for a minimum fee of $300,000 per appearance. The Saddam Hussein Library will be constructed and financed by all the unknown people and countries that supported me during my thirty-five year reign – you know who you are. I am to receive a $3 million book advance by Simon and Schuster. And I get to be a goodwill ambassador to any foreign country after it has been hit by a horrific natural disaster.

That's it. I think this is a very good deal, something the Americans can feel very comfortable with. Everybody is happy.

This bargain is entered into the record April 14, 2006.

STRENGTH IS POWER

POSTED BY: SADDAM H.   AT 7:42 PM   (109) COMMENTS   PERMALINK ✉

This is Don Rumsfeld, and I don't think the correct answer to this little brouhaha is going to come out of anything less than a full military solution.

I have been informed that you have ignored all my top-secret communiqués to extract you from your cell and reinstate you as President of Iraq. US Psy-Ops believes that you are signaling us that you are not happy with the suggested arrangements, so I am willing to up the ante. Not only will you receive your country back, but soon after, the United States will invade Iran. We'll give you half.

It will be just like the old days, you and me pal, a real win-win for everybody. All you have to do is just allow yourself to be freed by Sunni insurgents ;-) and promise never to reveal the plan!

To give us the old "thumbs up" do this on camera: grab your crotch, give two pelvic thrusts and finish with a cabbage patch into a running man.

Posted by: LordSith

view more comments

Life On Lock-Down

Daily Trial Entry:

I am the Steve McQueen of *The Great Escape* and Paul Newman of *Cool Hand Luke*. I am on lock-down. I got no beef with the straw boss walking the big yard. I have been here before. I'll do the time standing on my head or playing games, like Burt Reynolds in, *The Longest Yard* (the original not the remake. That one did the sucking).

I have my blog. I have my prayers. I have my routines.

Each morning, if it is not time to try me, then I wake, make my bed, scrub my underwear, brush the teeth, floss, pick, rinse, arrange furniture, wash underwear, re-arrange furniture, examine gums, comb hair, rinse underwear, re-make the bed, hang underwear to dry, use baby-wipes to clean plastic silverware, paper plate, napkins, tray, table, sink, bed frame, bars, floor, walls, light fixture. Then I eat breakfast, put on my underwear and Bedouin gown and go to the exercise yard for some fresh air.

I pretend to have an obsession for watering the concrete enclosure, but in fact I am tending a secret garden. It is not too much, but my beauties are growing strong. While I have been content with the occasional dandelion, I am hoping this spring will bring some broomsedge, bachelor's buttons, and cocklebur.

In my secret garden, there are many plants to tend. See how this one clings to the shadows. She is lovely and shy.

The highlight of my day comes when I play with my pets. Originally, I had a flying bug for a friend. He is no longer among the living. For some time, a spider was interesting to talk with. I found him in my bed. Disgusting creature! He is no longer with us either. I managed to move on and came to realize that ants, while somber creatures, are a fascination. But much like Iranians, they tend to swarm and overwhelm you. Eventually I decided to curtail their activities with a spray canister of bleach. They too have departed this mortal plane.

One day, I chanced upon what would become a love affair, much like I would have had with a horse or a dog. And I named them Uday and Qusay.

Uday, Qusay! Come quickly!
Ho Ho, I forget they are snails.

Look how they march up and down the exercise yard. It is
like a parade for me. I am so proud.

I have purchased for Uday a prostitute. It makes him happy.
Hopefully he will not kill this one too.

You see even on the lock-down, I am ruler of my universe and master of my domain. I shall rise again...

– Tomorrow morning at about 8:15 a.m.

STRENGTH IS POWER

POSTED BY: SADDAM H.   AT 8:51 AM   (0) COMMENTS   PERMALINK ✉

comments

Judge Judy Rocks

Daily Trial Entry:

Again today is another day waiting for the trial to resume. My life is one long postponement, like standing in the checkout of your local supermarket on Saturday morning when only two out of fifteen checkers are open. Very frustrating.

Not at all like Judge Judy. I might have a chance with her. She is fair and would listen politely to my side of things, as long as I did not make a speech. But with her, why would I?

Judge Judy would listen and then we would all go home. Maybe I would have to pay a small fine, but that would be okay ... I would give my interview in the hallway, call out the prosecutors, write my check to the bailiff, and it would all be over in 22 minutes. Now that is justice.

> **Judge Judy:** Mr. Hussein, can you please tell me your side of the story?
>
> **Me:** Yes your honor. I am the president of Iraq and some people were trying to kill me. I had them arrested and put them on trial. They were found guilty and suffered the punishment.
>
> **Judge Judy:** Do you have a receipt?
>
> **Me:** Yes, I do, your honor.
>
> **Judge Judy:** Okay, and you say you were murdered and tortured by Saddam?
>
> **Man Behind Curtain:** Yes, your honor...
>
> **Judge Judy:** Do you have a receipt?
>
> **Man Behind Curtain:** Yes, your honor.
>
> **Judge Judy:** Okay, we'll be right back with my verdict.

–Now that would be justice....

STRENGTH IS POWER

POSTED BY: SADDAM H.   AT 9:00 PM   (90) COMMENTS   PERMALINK ✉

This tribunal IS SLOW. With all of the formalities, it will take forever for this trial to finish. Slobodan Milsovic was on trial for nearly 5 years and we finally just poisoned him because nobody could take it any longer. At this pace your trial could go on for at least 20 years.

Even if you're found innocent, what will be left in 20 years? There won't be any Iraqis alive to govern. All the buildings will have been blown up. With the possible exception of a few palaces which I'm sure will have been turned into water parks or rented out for Weddings and Bar Mitzvahs.

Lets get on with it. You still have another two trials left!

Posted by: CIAguy

To CIAguy: Iraq will make a fine place to live 20 years from now. Shiite Mosques will be brimming with worshippers, a strong national government will serve the majority's interests, and a superior nuclear arsenal will protect its people from the Great Satan. And it doesn't hurt to be part of a much larger land mass.

As the President of Iran, this is the actual plan that I have drawn up. I also have plans for a car that runs on sand, a pair of giant sun glasses to cover the entire Middle East, and a pool on the moon.

Posted by: screwball

view more comments

If I Were A Danish

Daily Trial Entry:

My speech is not free. I stand and decry, "Who can believe this witness? If he blacked-out how can he remember if he was tortured?" I am not allowed to elaborate. I am told to sit down and stop making speeches! My speeches need freedom. Oh well, I am left to doodle.

– I should send these to a Danish newspaper they will print anything.

I ask you, which would you choose?

STRENGTH IS POWER

POSTED BY: SADDAM H.   AT 7:35 PM   (1) COMMENTS   PERMALINK ✉

comments

I just have a quick sec before I have to run out to my next violent protest. But I wanted to say great pic of JC – really funny stuff.

Posted by: JihadOnU

view more comments

Saddam's Final Solution
For Better Nutrition!

Daily Trial Entry

Some accusations being hurled in my direction are so outlandish. They are comical. These people have no idea how much I care for my subjects. Here is another example from today's trial:

. . . .

…Three sons had been held back in Abu Ghraib to face execution in 1985. The rest of the family eventually returned to Dujail to find its orchards of lemons, oranges, date palms, and pomegranates flattened by government bulldozers. "It became a desert," said al-Hattou. "I couldn't even find it because I didn't recognize the land."
– *Cox Wire Service*

. . . .

Of course I ordered the clearing of the orchards. This was a charitable act. At the time I was on the Atkins Diet, low carbs … and I was amazed at how much weight I had lost – *34 pounds* – eating nothing but beef ribs for six weeks and I felt great!

I thought if it worked for me, it could work for all Iraqis. But too much good land was devoted to carbs like figs, dates, and wheat. So I razed the land to make room for cattle so that all Iraqis could be lean. Those people in that village all lost a lot of weight.

So this wasn't ethnic cleansing, but more of an ethnic cleanse, a high protein fast. Whatever, it worked, and the town lost more than 12,000 pounds.

STRENGTH IS POWER

POSTED BY: SADDAM H.   AT 6:11 AM   (0) COMMENTS   PERMALINK ✉

comments

I'm with Simon & Schuster and I just have to say that the addition of posting advice to your blog is so very exciting. During a roundtable discussion on new titles, we came up with an idea I think you are going to love.

We are very interested in publishing a Saddam diet book. We are convinced that "The Saddam Hussein Diet" would be an instant hit. Here are some sample chapters:
Never Eat Again
What You Can't See Can't Make You Gain
No Arms, the Best Way to a Slimmer You
Who Needs a Tongue?
and
You Can't Eat When You're Hanging Upside Down by Your Testicles.

Please let us know; we're all very high on this title.

Posted by: ClaudiaReads

view more comments

Insane in the Hussein

Daily Trial Entry:

Finally a lucky break has been caught by me. One of the many men who were poking me and looking in places I have, came back to visit today. And I thought, "Uh oh, here we go again." But all he said was...

"I am the attending physician who examined you to determine if you were competent to stand trial, and after reading your blog, I realize I've made a horrible mistake. You are crazy."

And handed me this...

Dr. Stanley Finkelberg
Psychiatry and Psychoanalysis
Insanity Plea Specialist Since 1987
If you're behind bars and haven't called Stan...
Then You Are Crazy!
1-555-URCRAZY

S. Hussein

NAME _____ AGE ___
ADDRESS _____ DATE _____
Rx ILLEGAL IF NOT SAFETY BLUE BACKGROUND

℞ Formal Thought Dissorders:
- Schizophrenic
- Paranoid / Delusional
- Hallucinations "Talks to Snails!"
- Manic + Creepy
- MEDICATE IMMEDIATELY

Refil _____ times

DO NOT SUBSTITUTE [ ]

To ensure brand name dispensing, check and initial box.

So why am I still standing trial?! I'm at least as crazy as that guy in Afghanistan who converted to Christianity and was declared insane and shipped off to Italy. I am frigg'n NUTS COMPARED TO HIM; I re-embraced Islam.

Man converts to Christianity ... nuts!

Man converts to Islam... totally fuckin' nuts!

Man converts to Scientology... all right, you get the point.

I should be recuperating in Rome right now. I implore the international community to pressure my American oppressors to release me to Italy, now!

STRENGTH IS POWER

POSTED BY: SADDAM H.   AT 2:34 AM   (0) COMMENTS   PERMALINK ✉

comments

As a member of BlogPost, maintaining appropriate conduct consistent with our online community is part of your agreement with us. Your site has been flagged many times concerning detailed discussions on weapons of mass destruction, torture, killings, rape etc... Please be advised that your blog will be shutdown if you do not stop these posts at once.

If continued, this behavior may result in a fine or a possible prison sentence.

Posted by: costumer_relations

---

view more comments

THE SADDAM DUMP

[The End]

The Best Defense Is To Be Offensive

Daily Trial Entry:

I grow tired of being on the defense always. It is better to be offensive. I have just come from a meeting with my lawyers. We are suing and we have leaked it to the press…

. . . .

Saddam's Defense Sues Bush And Blair

Lawyers plan to file a law suit against the American president and the British prime minister in a European international court, on charges of illegally invading and occupying Iraq.

–Al Jazeera

Saddam To Sue Over Prison Photos

Saddam Hussein plans to take legal action after a British newspaper published photos of him half-naked in his prison cell and doing his washing.

- BBC

. . . .

I will sue them for every penny they are worth! I will sue them for defamation of character. I will sue them for wrongful termination and lost wages. Here is a ledger of my earnings for my last year of fulltime employment.

2002 Earnings Statement: Saddam Hussein	
Oil For Food Reallocation	1.2 Billion
Extortion	563 Million
Real Estate Acquisitions	354 Million
Interest, Swiss Bank Account	60 Million
Salary	12 Million
Pimping	8 Million
Xmas Bonus	250 Thousand
Total Earnings	2.2 Billion

I will sue them for discrimination. Look at this person they brought in to run things after me: couldn't speak the language, didn't act like us, didn't dress like us, really classic – white guy!

Can you spot the Head of the Coalition Provisional Authority?

I will sue Cheney, Rumsfeld, and Powell for copyright infringement, for use of my trademark phrases: WMD, mushroom cloud, smoking gun, and "By God, Harry was in the line of fire." Everyone knows I used those as justification to invade Iran years ago.

I will ask the ACLU to bring a class action suit against Bush and the United States on behalf of all Iraqis for damages caused to: palaces, underground bunkers, stretch limousines, statues of me standing, statues of my head, statues of me on horseback, giant murals of me, and spider hole entrance.

I am going to sue Bush so much I'll end up with the Crawford ranch, and the Kennebunkport offshore fishing boat. When I'm through with him he'll have to sign autographs at gun shows and conventions for the next 50 years just to cover the interest.

I wonder how much I can get for his flight suit on eBay.

Compensation is payable by check, money order, or Home Depot Club Card.

STRENGTH IS POWER

POSTED BY: SADDAM H.   **AT 10:11 PM**   **(0) COMMENTS**   **PERMALINK** ✉

   comments

The Green Zone is for loading and unloading of passengers only. Any unattended vehicle will be towed at owner's expense. Please report any unattended baggage to a security officer.

The Afterlife Awaits

Daily Trial Entry:

It is apparent that I could be hung for crimes that I did not commit. If this is to be my fate, I shall die a martyr for a great Islamic nation. Allah surely will reveal paradise and the seventy-two virgins who await me. But yet this is troubling. Is this really paradise for me? I've already had seventy-two virgins while frolicking in a gold-plated swimming pool filled with champagne as they massaged my groin area with fresh pomegranates.

Surely there's something more extravagant waiting for me. Do I get two hundred sixty-two Virgins, or something crazy like that? Seventy-two virgins are about max for what one man can handle in any given night.

It could be Allah's will that my paradise doesn't involve sex at all, but that I get to be in charge of a great and powerful country for all eternity. I would be the Celestial President of Ameri-qaeda. The great Ameri-qaeda artists would paint me and they would perform plays on my behalf at the Saddam Center. I would sit back in my special opera box and enjoy the first great Ameri-qaeda play: *Death of a Salesman, Carpenter, Camel Trader, Jeweler, Clothes-maker, and the Entire Northern Native Populations.*

I would have the great monuments bear my face, no matter how difficult it would be to carve a one hundred-fifty foot moustache into solid granite.

Great Ameri-qaeda songs would be composed in my honor:

> This land is my land,
> this land is my land,
> I think I'll take Thailand
> and the Virgin Islands

Being in charge of the world's most powerful army, I would immediately invade Nova Scotia. Then I would annex Greenland and demand control of Denmark; this would give me the gateway to Europe, which I would invade instantly. Once I had the world under my control, I would set my eyes towards outer space and then the beyond.

When I become the Celestial President of Ameri-Qaeda, my favorite artists will render my portrait.

Every four years I would reconfirm my Presidency with a giant political convention where all of my supporters would wear buttons, hold up signs and give out bumper stickers.

Whatever I wanted would be mine. Seventy-two virgins? Try having your choice of three and a half billion women at any given moment. I am Saddam Hussein, Celestial President of Ameri-qaeda!

– That would be awesome.

STRENGTH IS POWER

POSTED BY: SADDAM H.   AT 7:01 AM   (0) COMMENTS   PERMALINK ✉

comments

Saddam Phone Home

Daily Trial Entry:

We are wasting time with all of this "crimes against humanity," and "ethnic cleansing," yadda, yadda. I am thinking the chase needs to be cut. This trial is about justifying the invasion of my country. That is what we should be dealing with!

Was the invasion about WMD? No, I have no WMD – I used them all. Was the invasion about democracy? Yes, if you spell democracy H.A.L.L.I.B.U.R.T.O.N. Was the invasion about oil? Maybe, but they're pumping even less now.

So why invade me? I wasn't doing anything. I was minding my own business. Well, I have a theory. Today I was surfing the net and I came across this analysis of Zecharia Sitchin's book *Twelfth Planet*:

> All clandestine groups... may be jockeying for the best position, in a race for ET technology and knowledge. That may be necessary ... in a forthcoming ET confrontation/encounter ... that will determine the future of human civilization ... as we know it.
>
> Why is the United States in a hurry? Because Planet Nibiru ... may be coming! The Prize is owning and occupying the site of the Anunnaki's "home away from home" – Iraq

And this from the guys over at UFOroundup.com

> "Imagine this scenario. The U.S. government obtains intelligence that hidden somewhere in central Iraq is an actual stargate, placed there by the Anunnaki 'gods' of ancient Sumeria... In this scenario, when Nibiru (the alleged "twelfth planet"—J.T.) is closest to Earth, the Anunnaki" will "take the opportunity to travel to Earth through that same stargate and will set up their encampment in Iraq."
>
> "With time running out, President Bush invades Iraq. American scientists raid the (Iraqi national) museum and close the stargate,

> thus frustrating the grandiose ambitions of the self-styled reincarnation of Nebuchadnezzar, Saddam Hussein, and making the world safe for the New World Order."

Also from UFOroundup.com

> UFO Roundup correspondent Mohammed Hajj al-Amdar suggested that the prisoner-of-war in Doha (Hussein) "might perhaps be one of Saddam's clones, a creation of the aliens who befriended him before the war..." Mohammed still believes that "Saddam left Iraq long ago" and is now "living at an ET base on the moon with other humans and aliens."

A-ha! So I am either a clone or I've been taken to the moon by aliens. The Internet is such an amazing resource. Now I know why my country is illegally occupied.

This explains so much, like the fact that I cannot be killed. The Anunnaki must have given me immortality and super powers. S. – Saddam – S. M. – Supper Man, think about it!

I am locked in an eternal battle with my arch nemesis. The greatest super power the world has ever known and they could not defeat me. They even had their hands down my throat and yet I still live.

Alas, they know my only weakness. It is my kryptonite. It is how they have controlled and imprisoned me. I cannot resist the power of the Dorito. Damn.

– I should talk to my lawyers about another motion for change of venue, to the moon.

STRENGTH IS POWER

POSTED BY: SADDAM H. AT 6:00 AM   (0) COMMENTS   **PERMALINK** ✉

comments

Hitler, Stalin, Me

– Just thinking out loud here.

STRENGTH IS POWER

POSTED BY: SADDAM H.   AT 4:44 AM   (0) COMMENTS   PERMALINK ✉

comments

E-Mail Is The Tool Of The Devil

Note To Self:

I do not have trust in the emailings. They are a tool of the devil. Sometimes I lose them. Sometimes I wonder, "Who is this sender?" People are always saying to me, "Didn't you get my email?" Take for instance this one I received. How fantastic and wonderful it would be if it is real. I am not sure I can believe it.

Saddam,

I'm George W. Bush, President of the United States of America. The United States intended to give the Iraqi people a modern, free society; however, it has become apparent that too many of the Iraqi people are still living in the 12th century.

My generals inform me that even if we did everything right, it could take at least another 300 years to achieve our mission and that would just take us to the 15th century. And that's 15th century Iraq which is really like the 12th century anyway... so it would really take us 1200 years which is really like 2600 in Iraqi years for the US to be victorious. My advisors are not sure the American people have that kind of staying power.

We've calculated the loss of US Troops for such a protracted engagement at 228 million US troops dead and another 1 billion maimed or injured; the Iraqi casualties: everyone.

Although I've tried to convince our State Department and military generals that these numbers could be acceptable when stretched-out over 12 centuries they are not convinced. They inform me that I will be in office for only another 2 and half years, and that my popularity is lower than the ratings for Major League Baseball.

Therefore, I am prepared to offer you a deal. We will begin full withdrawal of our troops in the next 30 days after we announce that the Iraqi military can handle things – of course, you and I both know better. On the 21st day of the withdrawal at 0100 hours, our Sergeant Hollister with 12 of his men, I believe he's been in touch with you, will invade your holding area dressed as Iraqi insurgents.

You will be taken back to your main Palace in Basra, where you will be given your military uniform back, a razor (the beard has to go – only the moustache stays) and you will declare yourself President of Iraq. You will then be secretly handed control of the new Iraqi military. All we ask in return is that you continue to sell us the oil and don't bad mouth us too bad.

It's a very simple plan.

By the way, just out of curiosity, were there ever any WMDs? I think you can tell me after all that's happened. I won't tell anybody. I swear. For the love of God, you must tell me.

All right, that's the plan.

You see, very confusing. What if it's true? Should I send a reply in one email or address each question separately? Maybe highlighting my answers in his text will work best, or cutting and pasting his questions with my answers in a new file, and sending that as an attachment? How do I know my response won't be trapped in a spam filter? And what if he BCC'd the CIA or the IST or the NSA or my ISP? — I prefer to talk to a man to his face.

STRENGTH IS POWER

POSTED BY: SADDAM H.   **AT** 12:58 PM   (19) **COMMENTS**   **PERMALINK** ✉

comments

Dude, I get that all the time. Where's my email? Where's my email? Waa waa waa! UR a nimrod!!!

Posted By: Stoner_ITguy

You should disregard that email Saddam. It is clear to me that the "boys" have made another one of their tactical errors, one of thousands, I'm sure. We can't have American soldiers barging into an American detention center. What if we end up with casualties? Or someone has a camera, God forbid? No, I think I'm going to handle this one.

Here's how it will work. We declare you incompetent to stand trial because you are insane, which you obviously are. Then we commit you to a local psychiatric ward. Finally, we'll release you and reinstate you as President, just as soon as the media circus dies down, and the American public turns its attention towards the hottest new topic. Eventually they will forget all about you. Usually takes about 45 days.

Posted By: Condi4Prez

It's a real email. Who else talks like that except W? A regular fella I could have a beer with and all. But he's also really assured of his self. Makes me feel safe.

Posted By: Patriot01

---

view more comments

Saddam Is The One

Daily Trial Entry:

I have exciting news today. I can ignore this trial, because a higher judge has set me free. This morning while tending my garden, I was surprised to see one of my beauties burst into flame. As I watched in wonder, the fire burned bright, but did not consume the plant. Suddenly a voice began to speak as if inside my head, and lo it said unto me…

Voice Inside My Head: Saddam, you are the chosen one.

Me: Are you talking to me?

Voice: Is there anyone else here? I must be talking to you.

Me: Right.

Voice: Saddam, you are the one.

Me: You mean I'm Neo?

Voice: Ummm… Yea, sure Saddam you're Neo. Listen, you've had a nice run as the mortal visage of the anti-Christ, but your time on earth is drawing nye, and I need you to switch gears. Saddam, you are the Mahdi, the Muslim Messiah, the savior of Islam.

Me: Who is this again?

Voice: I am Yahweh, G_D, father to Jesus, Mohammad and Moses, Prince of Light, King of Kings, Omniscient and everlasting creator of all things heaven and earth.

Me: And?

Voice: And, to fulfill the prophecies you will be martyred, and suffer a painful death. You will rise from the dead and lead a purging of the unjust and wicked. You will impose on the land the rule of supreme law.

Fire and brimstone shall rain down. The earth and sea shall rise up and devour whole cities. Four horsemen shall ride down from the skies bringing war, famine, and plague and all of mankind will be laid low in your presence.

Me: Wow. Sounds like a Jerry Bruckheimer film!

Voice: Saddam, it will be much, much bigger.

Me: Cool – so why all the fuss?

Voice: This is evolution, Saddam, a second chance. For, when all of this has come to pass, the dark clouds of destruction will part, and Jesus will descend from heaven on layers of billowing satin. The sun will beam. Birds will sing. Dolphins will dance. The Mahdi and Christ will reign in harmony and bliss the rest of their natural lives — the world will be born again.

Me: You mean like G.W. did when he dropped the "Peruvian marching powder" and Dewar's diet?

Voice: Exactly.

– The flame went out.

STRENGTH IS POWER

POSTED BY: SADDAM H.   AT 3:58 AM   (122) COMMENTS   <u>PERMALINK</u> ✉

comments

Holy burning weed in your concrete exercise yard Batman, that's a lot to swallow! You know what I believe Saddam? I believe in churches because I can see them.

Posted by: Agnostic_Frontal_Lobotomy

<u>view more comments</u>

The Disco Messiah

Note To Self:

AMAZING! But where are the meanings? Is the matrix disintegrating? Jesus and me best buds? We get apocalyptic annihilation and raining fire with no rape or looting? And what's this about my painful death? – ouch.

So I pondered these many things and I kept them close, not even confiding in my guard sons or my cherished pets Uday and Qusay. And this is what I have come to understand...

Everyone is way too uptight! Especially God. We keep killing each other over and over and over and over and over and over again and for what? We worship the same omnipresent blah, blah whatever it was he said. Judaism, Christianity, and Islam share the same origins, scripture, and history. But we can't get along because of "faith?"

Bottom line: we need to give it an unwinding!

I think God is right. It is time for civilization, as we know it to end. And I am the one to get it done. But when God gets through with all that death and destruction business, Jesus and me are going to PAR-TAY!!!!!!

What are we waiting for?

From the holy book of

SADDAMISM

The One Saddamic Law: Do what you want!

The Saddam's Prayer

Our Leader, who art all powerful,

Hussein is Thy Name.

Thy Kingdom come, Thy Will be done,

Without delay or question to your supreme authority.

Give us this day our daily bread,

And some wine and cheese might be nice,

Forgive those who trespass against us, unless they're Jewish.

And lead us not into temptation too often,

But deliver us from evildoers and suiciders.

For thine are the disco, and the party, and the money,

Take me higher and higher.

SaddA-Men

The Sign Of The Noose

The sign of the noose is performed by taking the index finger of the right hand, as if pointing towards oneself, and encircling the face in a counter-clockwise fashion. Then, at the zenith of the second pass, making a fist, as if holding a rope, while making a yanking motion upward, and cocking the head to the left. Sticking the tongue out and crossing the eyes are optional but recommended.

MAY SADDAM BE WITH YOU

Coming in 2006 from

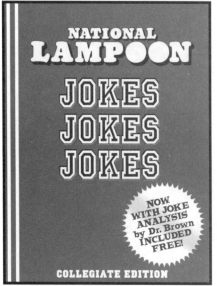